JOHN KEATS'S PORRIDGE

JOHN KEATS'S PORRIDGE

Favorite Recipes of American Poets

Victoria McCabe

UNIVERSITY OF IOWA PRESS

Library of Congress Cataloging in Publication Data

McCabe, Victoria, 1948–
    John Keats's porridge.

    Includes index.
    1. Cookery. 2. Poets, American I. Title.
TX715.M119   641.5'973   75–8612
ISBN 0–87745–058–7 pbk.

University of Iowa Press, Iowa City 52242

JOHN KEATS'S PORRIDGE is dedicated in fun and on a full belly to: R. P. Dickey and Shannon Dickey, Ray and Ruby McCabe, Mike, Dan, Mark, Tom, and Raymond McCabe, Syd and Mary LaMore, Delno and Naomi Dickey, Jim and Linda Taylor, K. T. and Ted Roes III, Duane and Debbie Clark, Michael Levine and Dee Myers, Dwight and Judy Frideres, Anna M. Buecker, Linda Harris, Ron and Becky Juelfs, and to all good poets and good cooks everywhere.

THE POETS & THE RECIPES

FOREWORD

THE WORD has always been that painters are the best cooks, but after reading this gorgeous gallimaufry I begin to wonder. Not that this is gourmet fare; it's mostly good solid eats, with plenty of nourishing stews and casseroles. There's a tradition of poets writing about food: I think of Swift, Thackeray, Burns, R. H. Barham, and, contemporaneously, Chesterton, Ogden Nash, and our own Erica Jong. For what can stir the soul more than a steaming dish of something delicious? Well, true love, perhaps. But true love, we're told, fleets, and a true stew can always be counted on. Good food exhilarates the young, and is the last remaining pleasure of the old.

There's nothing in this book I wouldn't eat except Herb Gold's "Prunes with White Sauce," which, on close examination, turns out to be prunes with milk, which I believe I've had enough of. Not, of course, that I would eat any of the concoctions submitted by the handful of jokers you find in any pack of poets—the puree of moonbeams, essence of sea spume, etc. I *did* eat the editor's recipe for gruel, and I will say that it *can* be eaten, but is much improved with Parmesan on top—as what isn't? I made Joe Kennedy's stew, and he's right, ". . . the Irish whiskey adds dignity." I like the thought, but have neither the time nor money to make this book's most elaborate recipe, Bill Smith's "Sonja's Choucroute."

I must say that, although it wasn't planned that way, this ends up being a pretty well-balanced cookbook. You've got your soups, your first courses, lots of entrees, breads, salad dressings, and desserts. And two straightforward recipes for mixing hard liquor and water. The emphasis, because of the geographical location of the editor, is on the cuisine of the Southwest, and that's O.K. with this eater since this Mexican-derived food is delicious, cheap, and filling — three requisites for a poet's food. I have edited a number of cookbooks, and I can say of this breed of book that most are not interesting reading. But poets? Ah, they use such phrases as May Swenson's "Serve and eat with a rounded (not pointed) silver spoon," and Richard Ellman's "Slice thinly into fully circumferenced slivers." And Don Hall's manly straightforwardness recommending Hellman's Mayonnaise in the East and Best Foods Mayonnaise in the West, and concluding, "If you use a salad dressing the mixture becomes poisonous, and leads to instant death." And I admire the way Miss McCabe lets the poets' lines stand as written; if one calls them "green onions" and another calls them "scallions," why, what matter? We know what they mean, and poetic license is allowed. There are some good laughs, and some nuggets of useful information, such as how to confront a Jerusalem artichoke, and what a Hanging Tenderloin is. As a long-time food book reader, I'd never heard of one. But I checked with my butcher, and *he* knew.

There's also some social content; commentary on what we've come to in this, supposedly, land of milk and honey. I think of Howard Nemerov's "Eggs Maledict," an indictment that reminds me of Billie Holiday's "Loveless Love," which I quote from memory, missing a word: "Such (something) times I never saw / That's why we need a pure food law / From milkless milk to silkless silk / We are getting used to so little."

This good anthology of recipes is as satisfying to this reader as a good anthology of poems, for after all, all recipes are poems to the hungry man.

New York, 1975   WILLIAM COLE

INTRODUCTION

What porridge had John Keats?
— Browning, "Popularity"

WHY A cookbook like this? It's common knowledge that poets visit one another: Poet A gives a reading at Poet B's University; Poet C reads Poet D's newest book and makes a pilgrimage to praise it; Poet E passes through Poet F's city en route to Grandmother's house. For one reason or another, poets get together at each other's homes. While he may not show you his new work, the poet host will inevitably invite you to try his homemade turtle soup with chives or his famous but secret original dessert. Being a poet myself, and being furthermore married to a poet, I have witnessed poetic celebrations in the kitchen that would rival the Cordon Bleu School for Chefs in ambition and intensity and excellence.

Randall Jarrell once wittily agreed with the charge that the "modern poet" was obscure — and insisted that his obscurity lies in the fact that virtually nobody reads him! *John Keats's Porridge* makes accessible to a wide audience many good, eminently readable recipes the poet/chefs wish to share. Poets cook for other people besides poets, of course. A lot of non-poets wonder about contemporary poetry, about contemporary poets and what they're up to. This book deals only with what some of them are up to in the kitchen, and it is a happy celebration of that activity.

Several of the poets contacted about this book remarked on the fact that there exists a kinship between the creation of a good meal and the making of a poem. "Good food is one of the major poetries of our lives," wrote one poet. So why has this book been so long in arriving? Admittedly my research is far from exhaustive, but to my knowledge there isn't a cookbook like it anywhere. There is one cookbook you see around which was written *for* poor poets, but not one written *by* poor poets, as most of *John Keats's Porridge* is. And who knows better the eating habits of poets than the poets themselves?

Aside from there existing a real need for this book, we must consider the deductions and summarizations sure to be reached in the future by some biographically-biased critics. After all, who knows what truths might be discovered about the poets of the Twentieth Century via knowledge of their favorite foods?

We know that bibles and cookbooks were among the earliest books printed. Each still outsells any of the other kinds of books. We also know about the sales appeal of poetry—probably the record holder in the opposite direction. Perhaps a marriage of the two will produce a happy medium: a book that will appeal to both the financially outcast poets and the socially affluent bookbuyers.

In late April of 1973, I mailed form letter requests to 250 contemporary American poets, asking them to send me their favorite recipe. I asked the poets to specify whether each recipe was an original, a variation on a standard recipe, or simply a favorite standard recipe. The general response was immediate and enthusiastic. For whatever reason or reasons, more than 100 poets did not respond to my invitation. Those who did respond were as excited about the project as I was.

"Fantastic!" wrote Donald Hall. "Are you sure you're not some projection of my imagination?" Hall was not the only poet to suggest that such a book had been lurking on the fringes of his imagination for years. "It's a natural," wrote Helen Sorrells, who added, "I love to cook!" Many of the poets who responded admitted that they were fairly great cooks when unleashed in the kitchen. Jim Harrison, expressing a common if unpoetic sentiment, wrote, "I've always been somewhat of a glutton so your note interested me a great deal." William Dickey wondered, "Why am I typing you a

recipe when what I really am supposed to be doing is grad-
ing term papers?"

Although Shelley states in "An Exhortation" that "poets'
food is love and fame," most of the recipes included here are
made of sturdier stuff. Breads and stews, for instance, run a
close race for all-time favorites. While not exactly poetic in
nature, the old Pennsylvania Dutch expression "Kissin'
wears out, cookery don't" seems more in tune with modern
poet-cooks. And nearly all of the poets align themselves with
E. E. Cummings who declared that American processed foods
are "Battle Creek seaweed." The reader of this cookbook will
find an abundance of "made-from-scratch" recipes. Some of
them, like John G. Neihardt's and Harold Witt's, have been
passed down through the ages within families.

It's interesting to note that nearly ninety per cent of all
the recipes submitted are either the poet's original recipe
or his variation on a standard recipe. Few poets, it would
seem, are willing to claim as favorite any old run of the mill
standard recipe. This is not surprising when we consider the
nature of the Beast: the poet as creator, inventor, who makes
out of a few necessary ingredients a magic potion. I think of
Mark Strand's "Eating Poems," a title which further suggests
an affinity between food and poets. And of course there's
Ezra Pound's well known statement: "The function of
literature . . . is precisely that it does incite humanity to
continue living; that it eases the mind of strain, and feeds
it, I mean definitely as *nutrition of impulse*." (Pound's
emphasis.)

All of the recipes included in this book *have* been tested—
by the poet-inventors themselves, by their guests, and by
your editor and her family. While there is no accounting for
personal tastes, each recipe is proven palatable to most and
poisonous to none (the exception being Don Hall's "Turkey
Amaryllis" which, as he warns, can turn on you lethally).

In all cases, the poets responded with thought and with the
conviction that it does matter what one eats. Not that the

whole thing—cooking, eating, and this book—isn't also a lot of fun, but I'm led to believe that most of them would agree with Samuel Johnson: "Some people have a foolish way of not minding, or pretending not to mind, what they eat. I mind my belly very studiously and very carefully."

While the majority of poets wrote that they love to create in the kitchen, several replied that their attempts in the culinary arts were limited to answering wives' calls to dinner. John Frederick Nims told us "I don't know how to cook anything except, on *rare* occasions, Campbell's soup." Others declared that their real favorite things to eat were either too expensive or too elaborate to be chosen as actual favorite recipes—which suggests that even (some) poets are practical. In fact, at least one half of the recipes submitted were chosen for their ability to keep a poor poet full for a long time without putting too large a dent in the pocketbook. Recipes such as Gene Warren's "Blue Jay Stew" and Ed Abbey's "Hardcase Survival Pinto Bean Sludge" are testimonials to the poet's imagination at work to beat monetary odds and still eat well.

Only about half a dozen recipes were written in the form of a poem—which might tend to support Louis Untermeyer's poem "Food and Drink" where he asks, "Why has our poetry eschewed / the rapture and response of food?" Although poetry in general may lack elaboration on food and food's joys, the poets themselves are well acquainted with all that: witness the comments most of them sent along with their recipes.

Many poets expressed regret that only one recipe per poet was allowed. True, it would have been interesting to read one poet's recipes for five hundred meals from one fifteen-pound turkey, and another's thirteen ways to dispose of one large hare—but space limitations prevail.

Although this book did not plan itself to become a traditional cookbook, it follows the traditional outline of soups, salads, entrees, and desserts. *John Keats's Porridge* is useful and will be at home in your kitchen. It is also entertaining. I can see it perched handily for visitors to thumb through, or reclining on an elegant coffee table, a collector's treasured item. I think you will agree that the book has varied charms — for which the poets and God's vegetables, meats, and sauces take credit.

For my part, I want to thank my husband, R. P. Dickey, for nudging me into completing the book and for willingly eating each new recipe. My mother, Ruby McCabe, started me out in the kitchen — for which I am now and forever grateful. And for the readers, a warm thank you for entering this zany kitchen. Happy eating your way through years of enjoying the favorite dishes of some of our nation's best poets.

JOHN KEATS'S PORRIDGE

Hardcase Survival Pinto Bean Sludge

1. Take one fifty-pound sack Colorado pinto beans. Remove stones, cockleburs, horseshit, etc. Wash in clear cold crick water. Soak for 24 hours in iron kettle or earthenware cooking pot. (DO NOT USE TEFLON, ALUMINUM, OR PYREX CONTAINER. THIS WARNING CANNOT BE OVER-STRESSED.)

2. Place kettle or pot with entire 50 lbs. of pinto beans on low fire and simmer for 24 hours. (DO NOT POUR OFF WATER IN WHICH BEANS HAVE BEEN IMMERSED. THIS IS IMPORTANT.) Fire must be of juniper, pinyon pine, mesquite, or ironwood; other fuels tend to modify the subtle flavor and delicate aroma of Pinto Bean Sludge.

3. DO NOT BOIL.

4. STIR VIGOROUSLY FROM TIME TO TIME WITH WOODEN SPOON OR IRON LADLE. (Do not disregard these instructions.)

5. After simmering on low fire for 24 hours, add one gallon green chile peppers. Stir vigorously. Add one quart natural (noniodized) pure sea salt. Add black pepper. Stir some more and throw in additional flavoring materials, as desired, such as old bacon rinds, corncobs, salt pork, kidney stones, ham hocks, sowbelly, saddle blankets, worn-out tennis shoes, cinch straps, whatnot, use your own judgment. Simmer an additional 24 hours.

6. Now ladle as many servings as desired from pot but do not remove pot from fire. Allow to simmer continuously,

for hours, days, or weeks if necessary, until all contents thoroughly consumed. Continue to stir vigorously, whenever in vicinity or whenever you think of it.

7. Serve Pinto Bean Sludge on large flat stones or on any convenient fairly level surface. Garnish liberally with parsley flakes. Slather generously with raw ketchup. Sprinkle with endive, anchovie crumbs and boiled cruets; eat hearty.

8. One potful Pinto Bean Sludge, as above specified, will feed one poet for two full weeks at a cost of about $11.45 at current prices. Annual costs less than $300.

9. The philosopher Pythagoras found flatulence incompatible with meditation and therefore urged his followers not to eat beans. I have found, however, that custom and thorough cooking will alleviate this problem.   ▓

Blythe Ayne

Stuffed Morels

8 med.-large morels	*Pepper*
1 lb. hamburger	*Onion salt*
½ green pepper	*Large can tomato sauce*
½ teaspoon salt	*Favorite cheese*

Fry off hamburger, add green pepper and spices. Roll morels in a little flour and salt. Deep fat fry briefly. Set on paper towels to absorb excess grease. Pour ½ of tomato sauce on hamburger. Stir. Lightly grease casserole dish. Carefully stuff hamburger mixture into morels. Place in casserole in two layers. Between layers and over the top pour the tomato sauce and lay slices of cheese. Bake in 350 degree oven for about 45 minutes.   ▓

Leonard Bird

Chicken in a Pot

1 teaspoon salt
1/4 teaspoon thyme, marjoram, celery, salt, & pepper
3 lb. boiler-fryer chicken (do not cut up)

Rub salt and herbs inside of whole chicken. Place in roaster with lid. Roast at 400 degrees for one hour or until tender. Serve with Rice Pilaf (see below).

Rice Pilaf

1 cup raw rice
1 cup chopped onion
1 cube butter

Brown together slowly. Add 2 cans beef or chicken broth (depending upon meat you serve). Bake covered at 300 degrees for 1 hour. Remove lid and bake at 325 degrees for another 1/2 hour. Add fresh or canned mushrooms (as much as you like) for the last 1/2 hour.

Besmilr Brigham

A Recipe That Is a Joy to Fix

Cut off fresh corn, cutting only slightly on outside of the grains, scrape the inside (like cut-up corn but without abundance of husk to grain). Put in a covered baking dish, add hunks of broken-up cheese, put in a little parsley, stir in an egg, and over this pour contents of one medium can of whole tomatoes. Bake at very low degree in oven in the covered dish. Oh, put in a little salt.

Roy says it's good.

23

John Malcolm Brinnin

Angolemono: Lemon Soup

To one quart of chicken broth (or fish stock) add two ounces of rice and boil until well-cooked. In a mixing bowl, beat up two eggs and the juice of two lemons. Once these ingredients are ready, slowness is all: spoon by spoon and stirring constantly, add four tablespoons of the boiling broth to the eggs and lemon. Add this mixture to the remaining broth and stir over a very slow fire for five minutes. Serves four.

Michael Dennis Browne

Fish Plaki

Wash a large fish, such as bream, chicken turbot, or John Dory. Sprinkle with pepper and salt and lemon juice, and put in a baking dish. Fry some onions, garlic, and plenty of parsley in olive oil; when the onions are soft add some peeled tomatoes. Fry gently for a few minutes, add a little water, simmer for a few minutes longer, cover fish with this mixture, add a glass of white wine, some more sliced tomatoes and thinly sliced lemon. Put all in a moderate oven and cook about 45 minutes or longer if the fish is large.

Hayden Carruth

Honest Countryman's Bread

6 cups lukewarm water
2 cups instant nonfat milk powder
4 eggs

6 tablespoons honey
2 tablespoons salt
2 tablespoons natural yeast (not *cakes*)

24

6 cups whole rye flour	*1 cup soy bean flour*
6 cups whole wheat flour	*About 6 cups white flour*

These ingredients are put together in the usual way. The yeast must be dissolved in one cup of the lukewarm water before it is added. I like to beat all of the ingredients except the flour with an eggbeater to be sure they are well mixed before I start adding flour. I add the whole grain flours first, then finish off with the white flour, kneading in as much as the dough will take without becoming too dry. It may run up to 8 cups of white flour sometimes, since I'm not always careful about measuring the liquid ingredients exactly.

Kneading should be long and vigorous. Then I let the dough rise once in a washtub, shape it into loaves, let it rise a second time in the loaf pans, then bake it somewhat slowly. I use a wood-fired oven and I'm not sure of the temperature. But I do know if you have the oven too hot you'll burn the outside before the insides of the loaves are baked through.

This recipe makes about 5 or 6 loaves, depending upon the size. I usually make round loaves and bake them in pie tins. Sometimes I add 2 or 3 handfuls of sesame seeds or sunflower seeds for a change of flavor. Sometimes I put in steel-cut oats and buckwheat. Please note that this recipe uses no shortening, no fat at all except what is in the eggs and the whole grains. It makes a solid but not heavy loaf with a rich, grainy flavor that I and my family like very much. This recipe is almost always reliable.

Hale Chatfield

Maya Casserole

1 lb. ground beef	*1 large can of tomatoes,*
2 tbsp. olive oil	*drained*

1 tbsp. raisins	1 cup water
½ cup chopped onions	1½ tsp. salt
1 cup uncooked rice	1½ tsp. paprika
⅓ cup green peppers, diced	½ tsp. Worcestershire
¼ cup dry sherry	sauce
1 apple, chopped	¼ tsp. black pepper
2 tbsp. chili powder	¼ tsp. celery salt

Brown the ground beef in the olive oil and remove from pan (a large casserole pan or Dutch oven). Add rice, peppers, and onions. Brown. Add all remaining ingredients and stir well. Boil briefly. Cover and bake at about 325 degrees for one hour. Four to six servings, preferably with a green leafy salad and red wine.

This recipe is a "favorite" in that it is inexpensive and relatively easy in preparation—and (I think) more zesty than most casseroles in its category. 🌼

L. D. Clark

Chicken Dumplings

Boil chicken until tender. Add salt to taste after chicken is tender. Then, add a dash of ground allspice or a couple of whole allspice. While chicken is boiling, make dumplings.

For dumplings for 1 whole chicken, take 4 eggs and beat well. Add 1 cup milk, and a dash of salt. Add enough flour to make stiff dough. Roll out dough and stretch very thin. Allow to dry and cut in squares. Drop dumplings in with chicken and cook dumplings until tender. Add top milk and black pepper. 🌼

Judson Crews

New Mexico Meat Loaf

1 lb. ground beef
1 cup mashed pinto beans
1 tablespoon New Mexico
 ground red chile
1 teaspoon cumin
1 teaspoon salt
1 can tomato sauce

1 fresh tomato, chopped
2 teaspoon sugar
1 tablespoon onion, chopped
1 small clove garlic, mashed
1 egg, slightly beaten
¹/₃ cup masa harina

Mix all ingredients in a bowl, shape into a loaf form in a shallow pan and bake in a preheated 350 degree oven for approximately 30 minutes. May be served with a chile salsa.

J. V. Cunningham

Chili

Pinto beans, as much as you want. Cook slowly, salt toward end. Brown meat—ground chuck, or lamb pieces cut up and simmered and skimmed, or diced pork—use a little flour if you like. Add tomato and chile (preferably pure, not the commercial powder) or use a can or two of canned tomato and green chile, adding as much more chile as you can take. Soy sauce or salt. Oregano, lots; cumin, about a quarter teaspoon per can of liquid; a pinch or two of coriander. Add chopped green onions and green pepper. Simmer.

Bruce Cutler

Recipe

    Lamb kidneys
    especially should be fresh
    and washed of course

ablutio with the white
membrane *caveat*
snipped away outside, inside;

tenuis but tenderly
split in half to clean
each hepatic hieroglyph

condiment with rosemary
and a very little salt
this being a form of prayer

but *in ultimo extremis*
try Jane's
Crazy Mixed-Up Salt

and broil
whatever you do
but briefly

or sauté
with a little onion, more sherry,
spices *supra:*

so it's lamb,
enjoy the pastoral.
Take it from there, Meliboeus.

Philip Dacey

Sour Cream Pancakes

¹/₂ cup sifted flour   *2 eggs*
¹/₂ teaspoon baking soda   *¹/₃ cup cottage cheese*
¹/₂ teaspoon salt   *³/₄ cup sour cream*

Put all ingredients into blender, cover, and process until well
blended. Let stand for 10 minutes. Bake on a buttered,

moderately hot griddle until brown. Turn only once. Yield: 8 to 10 pancakes.

These pancakes surpass all other pancakes because of their thinness. You *can't* make these thick. They have a very unheavy, unpancakey texture. They're pancakes for people who hate pancakes (and for people who love them, too). "Silken" is probably going too far, but it is going in the right direction. Great for the poet who does his writing in the morning and who wants something more than coffee and toast to help him face his blank paper. 🎖

Ann Darr
_____

Wild Strawberry Ice Cream

Wild strawberries	*³/₄ cup sugar*
2 eggs beaten	*¹/₈ teaspoon salt*
1 quart light cream	*1 tablespoon vanilla*

Chill freezer. Combine eggs, cream, sugar, salt, and vanilla. Pour into freezer can. Freeze until turning begins to be difficult. Open freezer can and add wild strawberries — as many as you can pick — or until the container has only room for the paddles. Freeze again until cranking is too hard, or until you are too hungry. 🎖

Joanne de Longchamps
_____

Western Short Ribs Casserole

About 6 pounds of beef short-rib cuts will feed four very hungry people. Trim all the excess fat and remove bones from meat, cut into inch squares and brown thoroughly on all sides in a heavy skillet, using no extra grease. Add a little salt and pepper. When the meat is browned, place in a large deep casserole or baking pan and sprinkle liberally with garlic salt. Over this arrange 2 diced medium onions and, if you like, some of the dried Italian mushrooms. Pour a No. 2 can of solid-pack tomatoes over all and place in a 350 degree oven for about 4 hrs.

This is an excellent dish to serve when the meal hour is uncertain, because it can stay, covered, in the oven for quite a while. About half an hour or so before serving, add a large can of cooked red kidney beans and garnish with small, canned, boiled onions. Cover the dish with aluminum foil for the last half of the baking period. Serve from the cooking dish.

This original recipe appeared in the SAN FRANCISCO CHRONICLE for November 27, 1955, and won me a check for $10.00. At that time, I could buy short ribs for 20¢ a pound!   ❀

Jerrell Dethrow
_____
Pork Tenderloin Martinee (Minus Gin or Vodka)

1 lb. pork tenderloin   *3 scallions*
1 8 oz. jar Green   *1 clove garlic*
   Giant Mushrooms   *1 bag of egg noodles*
½ cup dry vermouth

Slice tenderloin in ½ inch thick cubes, then flatten (via plate or meat hammer) to ⅓" pieces. Fry in butter for twenty minutes (over medium heat).

Meanwhile, dice garlic and scallions. Sauté garlic, scallions, and mushrooms; saving the liquid from the mushrooms.

After the pork has cooked 20 minutes, add vermouth, mushroom liquid, garlic, scallions, and mushrooms. Cook over low heat another 20 minutes.

Prepare egg noodles. Serve Pork Tenderloin Martinee over or aside noodles.

Serves 3–4.

James Dickey
_____

Cream Vichyssoise

6 leeks or 1¹/₂ cup minced onion	*3 cups boiling water*
	1 tsp. salt
3 cups white potatoes	

Combine above and cook 40 minutes. Put through a sieve and into a double boiler. Add:

4 chicken bouillon cubes	*1 cup milk*
3 tbsp. butter	*¹/₄ tsp. pepper*
1 cup heavy or light cream	*¹/₄ tsp. curry powder (optional)*

Heat until cubes and butter are melted. Place in covered bowl and chill. Garnish with chives, parsley, or whipped cream.

R. P. Dickey
_____

Beowulf Pancakes

1¹/₂ cups flour	*1 tablespoon sugar*
1¹/₂ teaspoons baking powder	*³/₄ teaspoon salt*

3 eggs	$^2/_3$ cup cream (Half-and-Half;
4 tablespoons melted butter	or, in a pinch, whole milk)
	$^1/_2$ cup malt liquor (or beer)

(Make sure your malt liquor has been uncapped and has set for at least two hours, eliminating the carbonation, before beginning.)

(An interesting variation is Beowulf Blue-corn pancakes, where, instead of regular flour, you use blue-corn meal.)

After the flour, baking powder, sugar, and salt have been measured into the bowl, stir in eggs, malt liquor, milk, and butter until the batter is pretty smooth. (You may choose to beat the eggs separately before stirring them in, but that is not necessary.) Grease your frying pan or griddle, heat it, and drop on enough batter to make your pancakes as large as you like them. Fry until bubbles appear generously on top, then turn and fry until browned up well.

Yields 10 to 12 average-sized pancakes.

Serve with a heated mixture of a little over $^1/_2$ honey, preferably unfiltered, and a little under $^1/_2$ malt liquor (or beer). As sauce is to spaghetti, this particular "syrup" is to Beowulf pancakes — or, for that matter, to *any* pancakes, including those made from Phil Dacey's superb recipe.

Then, as you savor these pancakes — and you will, even if you thought previously that you didn't like pancakes — think of Beowulf, Wiglaf, and the old mead halls.

The leftovers make choice nibbling, especially when they're cold, later on.   ✵

William Dickey

Garlic Chicken with Snow Peas

Peanut oil	2 quarter-size slices
2–3 scallions	of fresh ginger
2–3 cloves garlic	2 half breasts chicken

6–8 oz. snow peas (sugar peas, Chinese pod peas)
2 tbs. cooking sherry
2 tbs. soy sauce

1½ tbs. cornstarch
¼ tsp. Aji-no-moto (monosodium glutamate)

Stir-fry dishes work very fast at the last moment, so it is good to have everything prepared beforehand.

In a Chinese wok, deep electric skillet or frying pan, pour enough peanut oil to barely cover the bottom.

Cut the white part of two or three scallions in half-inch lengths. Peel and crush two or three cloves of garlic. Cut two rounds from a piece of fresh ginger and peel. Reserve.

Skin and bone two half breasts of chicken and cut the meat in half-inch dice. Tip and string the snow peas. Drop them into a large pot of boiling water and blanch them for two or three minutes only. It is essential that they remain crisp.

Mix together the sherry, soy sauce, cornstarch, and Aji-no-moto. Reserve.

Heat the skillet to hot, probably 375–400 degrees. In the hot oil, lightly brown the scallions, garlic, and ginger. When they are browned, push them to the side of the pan.

Add the diced chicken, and stir frantically, because it will stick to the bottom of the pan. In two or three minutes the chicken will lose its translucence and turn white.

Add the drained snow peas and again stir vigorously for two to three minutes. The only way to test this timing is to eat one of the snow peas. It ought not to be limp.

Pour in the mixture of sherry, soy, cornstarch, and Aji-no-moto, and again stir briskly, only until the cornstarch has absorbed the fluid of the pan: this will happen almost immediately.

As soon as the sauce has formed, remove the pan from the fire. Serve either over or with steamed or fried rice (over if

33

steamed, alongside if fried). Tea, sake, or a good Japanese beer is a better accompaniment than wine. And whatever our human and cultural fallibilities, this is a dish that should be eaten with chopsticks.

The only problem ingredients (and they become less of a problem every day) are the ginger and the snow peas. Snow peas can be got frozen. I have never made the dish with them; I would expect they should be blanched more briefly than the fresh peas. If fresh ginger is not available, I don't know quite what to do: you could try washing the sugar off crystallized ginger but would it work? Powdered ginger I don't think would do at all. All the other ingredients are readily available.

I've left the question of some ingredients open: I like garlic and I like to eat fresh ginger, but a lot of people don't: for them these subversive elements should be removed, before serving. The final product can be enriched with more soy sauce for those who have a good salty taste.

While I have never seen a recipe for this particular dish, it does follow the usual stir-fry pattern, and so all kinds of variants are possible. Relatively cheap cuts of beef can be used (bottom round, for instance), sliced paper thin, combined with asparagus or broccoli, and cooked with the same initial preparation and sauce.

While the quantities given here are intended to serve two, the recipe lends itself easily to being multiplied.

Albert Drake

Bud's Beanee-Weenee

1 28 oz. can pork & beans
3 wieners
1 medium sized onion
Tabasco sauce
Worcestershire sauce

Dump the beans in a kettle.
Slice the wieners and the onion.
Season.
Heat until it bubbles, then simmer for five minutes.

When I was small my father worked for a time in the WPA camp on Wolf Creek, in the coastal range, and before he'd leave, to be gone perhaps 2 weeks or more, he'd buy cases of soup and other canned goods for us.

One time he bought a case of Beanee-Weenee — a brand name I haven't seen since those days — which was simply beans with slivers of wieners. It takes a lot of eating to get through a case of anything, and I got to liking Beanee-Weenee.

This isn't my favorite food, but it's quick and filling, and I've been eating it for years. I'd rather eat fried razor clams and blackberry pie, but wouldn't know how to fix them.

Barbara Drake

Goulash

Chuck roast   *Sour cream*
Onions   *Noodles*
Paprika

This is a very snazzy looking and tasty too dish. *Not* a low cost recipe, however, as it takes a lot of meat.

Cut a good-sized beef chuck roast into bite-sized pieces. Cut off the fat, bone, tough spots, etc. Save these pieces for soup broth in another recipe (put them in the freezer or boil them and save the broth). Use only the lean pieces for the goulash.

Use a large, heavy pot (I like a cast iron Dutch oven) on top of the stove. Chop up about as many onions (in bulk) as you have meat. Sprinkle the onions and meat with enough paprika to coat them thoroughly. Stir them around a little.

Do not salt the goulash until it is done.

Cover the meat, onion, and paprika mixture with a tight lid (it makes its own juice—don't add water and don't let steam escape).

Cook on lowest temperature on stove burner several hours, about 3. *Don't try to hurry it* and *don't turn the temperature up* because it will boil dry or stick and the meat will turn out tough and it won't be the same thing at all. The onions and the chuck roast will make a great deal of good, thick meat juice and everything will be done when it falls apart and is utterly tender.

Serve over hot noodles, with sour cream, salt, and fresh pepper. (With bread, wine, and salad.)   ▨

Donald F. Drummond

Oysters Rockefeller

Allow 6 oysters on the half shell per person. Fresh spinach, cooked. (Don't cook very long, about 3 minutes is enough to get it limp.) Cream some butter with onion juice.

Cook oysters about 10 minutes at 450 degrees. Pile cooked spinach on top of oysters. Pile some bacon on top of the spinach. Put bread crumbs on top of the bacon. Pour butter/onion juice over all and there it is.

If you want Parmesan cheese over the whole thing, that's okay too.

This is very very very good; I first had it in New Orleans.

Alan Dugan
_____

My Recipe is This:

1. Boil two skinless frankfurters until they explode.

2. Cook one can of Campbell's beans in a sauce pan until the juice bubbles.

3. Fry two pieces of buttered bread in a frying pan until the crust of the bread turns black.

4. Dump products of 1, 2, and 3 into a soup bowl.

5. Add one green chili pepper or one new green pickle, according to taste.

6. Cover frankfurters with Gulden's Mustard, the sweet, yellow kind, and Heinz's Katsup.

7. Eat with a quart of cold beer.

Serves: one for lunch.
Result: Sleep and dysentery.

Stephen Dunn
_____

Rumaki

Chicken livers   *Water chestnuts*
Bacon   *Brown sugar*

Cut chicken livers and water chestnuts into bite-sized pieces and bacon strips into thirds. On toothpicks, spear each piece of chicken liver with a piece of water chestnut and wrap securely with bacon. Place spears on baking sheet and sprinkle with brown sugar. Broil until bacon is crisp.

Serve with a small bowl of hot mustard mixed with soy sauce to taste.

Richard Eberhart

Jerusalem Artichokes

1 lb. Jerusalem artichokes	*1 large onion*
¼ lb. grated cheese	*Whole wheat bread crumbs*
3 tbsp. butter	*Salt and pepper*

Steam artichokes until tender. Slice and place in casserole. Cover with sautéed onion, a layer of cheese, then bread crumbs. Dot with butter. Brown in a hot oven, 10–15 minutes.

Jerusalem artichokes are starchless, and highly nutritious. When some friends gave us about 15 surplus pounds of artichokes they grew, we had them for lunch for several days! The rest we fed to the goats, who love them. We had wanted to plant some to have our own patch, but didn't get around to it this year.

Jessie Ellison

Quick Spanish Bean Salad

1 can mixed yellow and green bean (snaps)	*1 can garbanzos*
	1 can kidney beans

1 sweet onion, sliced into rings	Dash of white cider vinegar
1 garlic bud	to taste
1/2 cup salad oil	Touch of freshly ground
1/2 cup Tarragon vinegar	black pepper to taste

Chop up garlic bud and place in mixture of vinegar and oil, together with onion rings. Leave until vinegar and oil have become flavored, then strain out garlic buds. Mix all beans with onions and oil dressing. Mix thoroughly, then chill until time to serve. Use wooden salad bowl and servers. ▨

Richard Ellman

Tomatoes Vinaigrette

Take a big fat red soft Jersey beefsteak tomato, about 1½ pounds, and a dozen small yellow Italian pear tomatoes, and slice thinly into fully circumferenced slivers. Place in a large tureen.

Add two pints French wine vinegar with tarragon. Smash in one clove of garlic and stir. Let sit for fifteen minutes. Add fresh dill, and parsley.

Chop the fine green ends of scallions into approximately quarter of an inch units and sprinkle generously. Add sliced pieces, or cubits, of red onion to taste.

Chill for approximately one hour, and serve with crusts of day old French bread, or pumpernickel, for dunking, and sweet butter.

Beverage to taste. But I usually drink Alsatian, or Dos Xs (Mexican) beer.

This is very refreshing for summer, and filling, too. Serves 2–3. ▨

Ossie Onuora Enekwe

(Pepper soup is not all that peppery as the name might suggest. The reason why it seems so is because it is usually taken while still hot. There is one consolation, though, for those who are still scared. They can decide just what amount of pepper to add, without depleting the rich flavor of the soup.)

4 pieces of chicken (thighs and breasts) liver, neck, breastbone, cut and crushed	1 onion, chopped $1^{1}/_{2}$ teaspoon salt 1 tablespoon pepper, coarsely ground
1 tomato, sliced	2 tablespoons tomato sauce
1 green pepper, sliced	

Wash the chicken pieces and without drying put them in a pot without water. Sprinkle with salt and turn on high heat. The chicken will give its own juice and take a nice gold color. When you have enough liquid, add sliced tomato and pepper, chopped onion and tomato sauce to give color. Turn on medium heat and cook 15–20 minutes. Serve the soup with the chicken pieces and eat when still hot.

Theodore Enslin

Lamb Spare Ribs Sweet and Sour

The entire rib cage of one small sheep (or lamb)	Several crushed star anise seeds
Vinegar	A few drops oyster sauce
Water	Salt, pepper
One cup soy sauce	One pint cooked greens
Two tablespoons raw sugar	(michihili, chard, etc.)

40

Put the ribs in a large pot. Cover with water to which has been added a liberal quantity of vinegar. Boil down slowly to the point where there is about one cup of liquid left.

Separate ribs. They will be extremely tender at this point. Place in a large frying pan, add soy sauce, more vinegar (probably ¼ cup or so), anise, oyster sauce, salt, and pepper.

Simmer for 10 minutes. Add cooked greens. Then simmer for ten more minutes. Eat immediately.

Serves approximately four people. This recipe is an original.

Dave Etter

Fresh Peach Wrinkle

8 medium-size peaches	*¼ cup milk*
2 cups sugar	*¾ cup flour*
2 tablespoons butter	*⅛ teaspoon salt*
1 egg	*2 teaspoons baking powder*

Pare and slice peaches. Place in shallow glass (or granite) dish. Allow to stand until juice is formed. Cream 2 table-spoons butter. Add slowly 2 cups sugar. Add 1 egg and beat thoroughly. Add alternately ¼ cup milk and ¾ cup flour sifted with ⅛ teaspoon salt and 2 teaspoons baking powder.

Place batter over peaches and cook for 45 minutes in oven set at 275 degrees.

Serve with whipped cream or ice cream. This original recipe will serve 6.

41

William Everson

The Hanging Tenderloin

The Hanging Tenderloin is the only part of the steer combining the tastiness of sirloin and the tenderness of filet mignon. It is rarely featured commercially because, like all excellent things, there is not much of it, and this very rarity renders it unmarketable. In the natural course of events more often than not it ends up ground beef, but if you ask it will be saved for you, and it is not expensive. Butchers themselves know its distinction, and cunningly carry it home, thereby earning for it its other, more prestigious name: The Butcher's Cut. Drivers of meat vans are notoriously sly in this regard. Since the piece hangs free in the animal, and can be deftly removed, many a carcass of beef is delivered to the retailer sans The Hanging Tenderloin.

In appearance it is a large, tongue-like muscle, eight to ten inches long, running three or four inches wide, and weighing around a pound and a half. There is a powerful sinew down the center; when removed this leaves two longish strips rather triangular in shape. Cut both strips across to make four manageable pieces and grill. If camping in the West, broil over living coals, the thick bark of Douglas fir burned down to pure embers, smokeless but marvelously aromatic. There is no experience of meat to surpass it. ※

Foster Robertson Foreman

Odd-Flavored Chicken with Almonds and Mushrooms

Into a deep pot with enough boiling water to cover put a whole, cleaned chicken. Bring to a boil again, turn heat to simmer and, making sure the cover of the pot does not come off for the next hour and a half, simmer for twenty minutes and leave with the heat off to steam for an hour.

Reserving broth for more enriching, separate the meat from the skin and bones, and pile the shredded and tender meat on a good plate or bowl.

(Put broken bones into broth and simmer again for stock to use for cooking rice today and for making avgolemo tomorrow.)

Prepare in a frying pan 2 tablespoons of vegetable oil and 1 T. of sesame seed oil, 2 chopped green onions, a thumb joint of sliced ginger root, and some crushed red pepper or fresh chile. Into this pan add a good handful of fresh sliced mushrooms and a small handful of almonds. Set aside.

In another bowl, prepare 3 T. of dark soy, 2 T. of honey, 1 clove of crushed garlic, and $1/2$ t. of salt.

Just before sitting down to eat, after cooking rice but before singeing fresh greens to eat with this:

Sauté the contents of the frying pan, add to the contents of the bowl, let sit a minute. Then toss the chicken shreds into this mixture, and enjoy! ✻

Paul Foreman

Szechuan (Texas TO-FU, Beancake)

*$1/2$ lb. country sausage
(ground)*
1 lb. fine white soybean cake
*A generous dash of ground
red pepper or $1/2$ of a fresh
hot red pepper chopped fine*
*2 or 3 teaspoons of Chinese
black bean sauce, depending
upon piquancy of taste*

1 lemon sliced in half
1 handful of brown sugar
*1 vegetable if desired,
preferably either a few green
onions or fresh mushrooms,
sliced fine*
Cornstarch as desired

To make: drop the sausage in thumb-sized balls into a hot skillet. Turn until cooked. Pour off the grease. Add the soybean cake and dice into chunks. Lower the heat to medium. Add pepper and beancake. Stir. Add the sliced onions and brown sugar. Raise the temperature to medium-high. Squeeze the two lemon halves into the mix and stir. Add cornstarch to thicken the sauce only if desired. Serve piping hot over boiled rice and stand by with cool water. Serves four.

Increase ingredients as desired. Some like it hotter. A Chinese roommate at Berkeley several years ago taught me this recipe. The lemon juice is my addition.

Robert Francis

Bob's Health Bombs (Bursting with Nutrition)

1. Blend roughly equal portions of high-grade raw honey and pure peanut butter.

2. Flavor to taste with vanilla.

3. Stir into the mixture wheat germ and, in lesser amounts, sunflower seeds, uncooked rolled oats (or granola), and powdered skim milk until mixture becomes almost too stiff to work.

4. Pick up lumps of the mixture and roll briskly between both palms held flat, to form balls an inch or less in diameter.

5. Roll balls in finely shredded coconut until well coated.

6. Refrigerate for firmness until ready to eat.

Bob's Health Bombs are the result of a challenge I gave myself some time ago. Could I invent a healthful confection out of the ingredients I keep on hand from our local natural foods store?

Martha Friedberg

Chicken en Vin Ordinaire

Salt and cover a cut-up fryer in lemon juice, fresh dill and any cheap, light, dry, beautiful white wine for a couple of hours. Then dip each piece into melted butter or margarine or a combination of both. Place in a baking dish in a 350 degree oven for an hour and then brown quickly at 450 degrees just before serving.

Allen Ginsberg

Borsht

Boil 2 big bunches of chopped beets and beet greens for one hour in two quarts of water with a little salt and a bay leaf, and one cup of sugar as for lemonade. When cooked, add enough lemon to balance the sugar, as for lemonade (4 or 5 lemons or more).

Icy chill; serve with hot boiled potatoes on side and a dollop of sour cream in middle of red cold beet soup. On side also: spring salad (tomatoes, onions, lettuce, radishes, cucumbers).

Herbert Gold

Prunes with White Sauce

Soak prunes in boiling water.

Heat milk.

Pour milk on prunes.

Suitable for breakfast, lunch, dinner, or *Walpurgis Nacht* Snack.

Turkey Salad Amaryllis

Take 2 pounds of cooked turkey meat, mixed white and dark. Chop into little pieces, of $\frac{1}{4}$ to $\frac{1}{2}$ inch, cubed.

Chop 2 cups of celery, about $\frac{1}{4}$ inch cubes.

Chop 3 cups of purple onions, $\frac{1}{4}$ inch cubed.

Chop $1\frac{1}{2}$ cups of green pepper, fresh.

Hard boil 6 large eggs, and pulverize.

Wash $\frac{1}{2}$ pound of mushrooms in water and vinegar. Clean further. Cut in large pieces. Nothing larger than a quarter in circumference.

Mix.

Add 3 tablespoons of basil. Very important.

Add a pinch of anise.

Add a pinch of dried mustard.

Add a tablespoon of salt, and a teaspoon of pepper.

Add 2 teaspoons of white tarragon vinegar.

Add $1\frac{1}{2}$ teaspoons of maple syrup.

Add a pint of Hellman's Mayonnaise. In the West, use Best Foods. Never use any other mayonnaise, not Krafts, or anything else. And if you use a salad dressing the mixture becomes poisonous, and leads to instant death.

Mix. Serve on leaf lettuce, with either tomato aspic or quartered fresh tomatoes, alongside, for beauty.

Serve with Miracle Beans. I would like to give the recipe for Miracle Beans, but they won't let me give more than one recipe.

Daniel Halpern

A Special Tagine Recipe

Ingredients

1 chicken (4 pounds)	4 large Spanish onions,
Salt	sliced lengthwise
Ground pepper	1 tablespoon ginger
4 tablespoons freshly ground	1 cup whole blanched almonds
cumin	Olive oil—the crudest
1 pound pitted prunes	you can find
3 tablespoons ground	
cinnamon	

Paraphernalia

2-quart saucepan
5½-quart casserole
Skillet

Serves 4

1. Cut the chicken into pieces. Rub salt, pepper, and cumin under the skin of the chicken and over the skin of the chicken. Be generous with the cumin—it's the personality of this dish. Let the chicken sit an hour.

2. In a saucepan, cover the prunes with cold water, add the cinnamon, and bring to a boil. Reduce heat and simmer 30 minutes.

3. Cook the onions in olive oil, ginger, salt, and pepper till clear. Not too long.

4. Meanwhile, brown the almonds in the oil, remove and drain on paper towel. Brown the chicken evenly on all sides in the same oil, adding ½ cup of water. Sprinkle with remaining cumin, cover and simmer for 30 minutes.

5. Add the cooked prunes and some of the prune water to

the casserole and continue cooking until the chicken and prunes are tender.

6. TO SERVE: Arrange the chicken breast in the center of the serving dish, place the legs and wings around it, and cover all with prunes and sauce. Sprinkle with the almonds and serve at once. Oh, at once.

I learned this recipe from Paul Bowles, who in turn learned it from Mohammed Mrabet, storyteller and cook par excellance. Acknowledgments also go to Paula Wolfert, author of *Couscous and Other Good Food from Morocco*, in which this recipe appeared in a slightly altered form. ▨

Jim Harrison
___

A Sort of Purist-Type Chili

Brown 5 pounds of cubed choice chuck (inch square pieces) in the fat rendered from good bacon. Brown lightly fifteen whole cloves of garlic. Add tablespoon of cumin and one-half cup of first rate Mexican chili powder. Add four dried red chili peppers and one pound of dry pinto beans. Cover with water. Add salt and a teaspoon of sugar and one small can of Contadina tomato paste for a binder. Cook at least eight hours at a simmer one day. Eat the next day with either freshly made tortillas or commercial ones. Have bowls of lemon wedges and chopped onion, cases of beer and gallons of good inexpensive Burgundy (I prefer Gallo Hearty Burgundy, as I'm a very poor poet). ▨

James Hearst
___

Beef Stroganoff

2 lbs. good grade round steak, $\frac{1}{2}$ lb. fresh mushrooms (or canned). Trim steak closely, trim away fat and connecting tissue. Cut in pieces an inch long, $\frac{1}{2}$ inch wide. Marinate

the meat over night in a ¹/₂ cup sherry, 1 cup sour cream. When ready to cook, remove from liquid, brown each piece lightly, then place in a pot or iron skillet, add liquid, add mushrooms sliced, cook for 2¹/₂ hours in the oven. Add more sherry if necessary. Serve on toast squares or on rice. Serves six.

I've made this for years; it is almost foolproof.

Daniel Hoffman

Coq au Chambertin

Decouper le poulet en morceaux—Faire revenir la viande dans une cocotte et ajouter une vingtaine de petitis lardons et autant de petite oignons—Quand le tout est roussi, saupoudrer d'une cuilleree de farine—Laisser roussir et ajoute une bouteille de vin rouge de Bourgogne—Assaisonner Couvrir et cuire doucement pendant ³/₄ h. a l heure.

Degraisser la sauce—On peut la lier avec le sang du poulet au dernier moment—Servir saupoudre de persil.

My wife attended *l'Ecole Menagere de Dijon* during a year we spent in France, and learned what is served at the table of the eternals: Coq au Chambertin.

John Hollander

Potage du Soir Carroll

In 6 qts. of dew, simmer together: a good-sized shank of the afternoon, a peeled shadow, some exhaustion, and a *bouquet garni* of pillow, litany, oaten stop and, if available, sullen horn. Before serving, stir in green going, to taste. A beautiful soup.

Anselm Hollo

Good Stuff Cookies

2 gods
²/₃ cup hidden psychic reality
2 teaspoons real world
³/₄ cup sleep

2 cups sifted all-purpose
 iridescence
2 teaspoons good stuff
¹/₂ teaspoon pomp & pleasure

beat gods hidden psychic reality
real world and sleep together
sift together iridescence — good stuff
pomp & pleasure
add to real world mixture

drop by teaspoon
2 inches apart — on cookie sheet
press cookies flat
with bottom of glass — dipped in sleep
bake at 400 F
8 to 10 minutes
2 dozen cookies — good stuff

Richard Howard

Creamed Spinach

Wash (in several waters) enough fresh spinach for six. Cook
in salted water until it smells like spinach. Put through the
blender (coarse), after squeezing out all the water you can.
MEANWHILE melt a quarter of a pound of butter and stir in
a lot of fresh-ground pepper and a very little pressed garlic.
Then gradually stir in the spinach until the whole mass is
of a single consistency. Then add one container (one pint) of
sour cream, stirring until the entire mass is the color of the
most expensive jade. Season to taste (a dash of Worcester-

shire sauce is likely, and cayenne), and keep hot in the
double boiler until ready to serve—can be made early in the
afternoon.   ▓

Richard Hugo
_____

Fettucine Verde al Forno

1 *lb. green fettucine or*	2 *green peppers*
flat spinach egg noodles	*Olive oil*
2¹/₂ *lb. prime lean ground*	5 *cloves garlic*
round	40 *oz. tomato sauce*
2 *large onions*	32 *oz. tomato paste*
2 *carrots*	16 *oz. canned mushrooms*
3 *celery stalks*	2 *lb. mozzarella, sliced*

A basic casserole, similar to lasagne, but not as rich with
the thinner noodle, and the ricotta left out. Except for a
handful of brands, American pasta is very bad and while
no gourmet, I find imported pasta is almost essential to any
Italian dish. Good cheese helps.

Brown and crumble meat in olive oil over medium heat.
Add ¹/₂ cup more olive oil. Add onions, carrots, celery and
green peppers cut into fine pieces (if you want some solidity
of bite, cut the celery into somewhat larger pieces than the
other vegetables). Add sauce and paste. Cook about three
hours at fairly slow heat. When the sauce is ready the pockets
of olive oil on the top should be a rich golden brown. At the
end of the second hour, add the garlic, each clove cut into
three or four pieces. Season during the last hour, as desired.
Salt will be necessary. Oregano always works. Thyme's O.K.
I'm against bay leaf. Rosemary is a possibility. The advantage
of Italian cooking, of course, is that you can slop it together,

as long as you observe the basics, spice as you wish, not adhere rigidly to timing (except for the pasta).

Cook noodles in already violently boiling water for 8 to 10 minutes. You can check to make sure the noodle isn't too hard. One advantage of Italian pasta is that if you cook it a minute too long it doesn't remind you of Wheaties left in milk five hours. But you should try to take it off while still firm.

In a large baking dish, place a layer of sauce on the bottom. Add a layer of noodles. Add a layer of sauce. Sprinkle the sauce with mushrooms. Cover with mozzarella. From then on, layer as follows: noodles, sauce, mushrooms, cheese. Sprinkle final layer with parmagiana if you want. Bake 45 minutes at 325 degrees.

This should serve 12 moderate, well-behaved couples, or six hungry drunk poets. If you want to get fancy, you can add to the sauce layers in the baking dish. Some possibilities: whole kernel corn, olives, pepperoni, sliced hard boiled eggs, etc. If you want fresh mushrooms, you can cook them in the sauce the last hour of simmering.

If you have plenty left over, warm only what you want to eat each time. Don't keep heating and reheating the entire dish. Don't heat after the fourth day unless the dish has been frozen. Olive oil in leftover food starts having poor effects on your system. This recipe is my variation on the standard Fettucine recipe.   ✹

David Ignatow

Bonac Fish Loaf

$1^1/_2$ cups cooked fish
$1^1/_2$ cups bread cubes

$1/_8$ tsp. pepper
$1/_8$ tsp. dry mustard

Dash of salt and paprika
2 tbsp. butter
1 cup milk

2 eggs, beaten
1 granted onion

Bake 45 minutes, oven 350 degrees. Serves 4.

Flake fish in bowl, add bread crumbs, onion, and milk. Mix well. Bake in buttered pan until golden brown.

(A simple and very appetising way to cook fresh codfish is to boil it—adding a little vinegar, a bay leaf and fresh pepper to the water.)

This recipe is by Mrs. John H. Mahoney of East Hampton and was taken from the 70th Anniversary Cook Book compiled by the Ladies Village Improvement Society of East Hampton, Long Island. ✺

Colette Inez
_____

Kung Fu Fish Slices

1 lb. filet of flounder,
* or any firm white meat fish*
1 tbsp. lard (leftover bacon
* grease for more pizzazz)*
$^1/_2$ tsp. salt
$1^1/_3$ tbsp. water
$^1/_3$ tbsp. cornstarch for fish mix
$^1/_2$ tbsp. cornstarch for paste
1 large egg white (save yolk
* to mix into morning orange*
* juice)*

$^1/_3$ tbsp. sherry wine
* (cheap cooking type will do)*
1 scallion cut into 1-inch
* slices, or blithely chopped,*
* as you wish*
1 slice dried ginger (better
* if it's fresh, but isn't it*
* always?)*

1. Cut each filet into 3 or 4 pieces. Mix with a sprinkle of salt, $\frac{1}{3}$ tbsp. cornstarch, and egg white.

2. Heat lard until hot, add fish and fry about two minutes on each side.

3. Blend paste with $\frac{1}{2}$ tbsp. cornstarch, sherry wine, scallions, ginger, and water. Add to fish.

4. Cook fish slices for two more minutes on each side, turning fish tenderly. Liquid becomes translucent, God willing.

Recipe should serve two hearties on the ranch, or three picky eaters. This fish dish is fit for King of the Ranch House and Other Ranges.   ✿

Dan Jaffe

Potato Latkes (Jewish Potato Pancakes)

2 eggs
3 cups grated potatoes
$\frac{1}{3}$ cup grated onion
3 tbs. flour
$1\frac{1}{2}$ tsp. garlic salt

$\frac{1}{2}$ tsp. chopped parsley
$\frac{1}{2}$ tsp. rosemary leaves
$\frac{1}{4}$ tsp. ground sage
$\frac{1}{4}$ tsp. fresh ground pepper
Vegetable oil

1. Beat eggs till light and foamy. Use an electric mixer on medium.

2. Stir in potatoes, onions, flour, seasonings, & herbs until thoroughly blended.

3. Heat $\frac{1}{4}$" of oil in a large skillet.

4. Drop batter by the tablespoonful and fry on each side until golden brown.

5. Drain excess oil by placing the latkes on paper towels for one minute before serving with sour cream or applesauce.

This recipe is my wife's; I can't cook anything more complicated than a Western Omelette! ✻

Donald Justice

Cheese Spread

Chop about ½ lb. medium sharp cheddar, 4 oz. pimentos, and about ⅓ cup mixed sweet pickles. Bind with mayonnaise, and salt to taste.

This was a recipe my mother must have worked up from somewhere. I know it sustained me through childhood and is still my favorite sandwich filling. ✻

Shirley Kaufman

Green Goddess Salad Dressing

½ pt. Best Foods Mayonnaise
½ cup tarragon vinegar
1 tin of flat anchovies
1 green onion

1 hard-boiled egg
1 tbsp. Worcestershire sauce
1 tbsp. cracked black pepper

Gradually stir vinegar into mayonnaise. Chop together onion, egg, and anchovies. Add to mayonnaise and vinegar with pepper and Worcestershire sauce. Mix well and refrigerate for several hours. Serves 12–14.

Combine 3 kinds of lettuce (butter, red, and romaine), enough to serve 12–14, in large salad bowl. Add a cup of chopped parsley and a cup of green onions. Toss with dressing just before serving.   ▓

Robert Kelly

Hisperic Pork

What I most like to eat is what Helen cooks, and then what I cook for her. Since *poet* means *maker,* and making is not isolate, not isolating, I offer a recipe from the second category, one I made up, though recently I've heard that the natives of Tuscany use a similar technique to tame the dragon in the pig. Before them, the Albigensian layfolk must have known these shifts. All making is making, and all work feeds the process.

Fry in 2 tbs. olive oil:

2 tbs. ground coriander (preferably freshly ground from heated seeds)
1 tsp. ground cumin
3 cloves of garlic, sliced fine
2 red chili peppers (optional)

After the garlic is browned and the peppers are blackening, add:

2 lbs. shoulder of pork, in ¹/₂ - inch cubes

Brown the pork for 5 minutes over medium heat. Remove peppers. Now pour into the pan all at once:

1 cup fresh milk

Stand back lest it splatter. Scrape the pan and keep the pork moving till the milk begins to boil. Add:

$1/_2$ tsp. salt

Lower the heat, cover tightly, and cook over lowest heat till the pork is tender, ca. 1–1$1/_2$ hours.

Stir every twenty minutes or so. More milk should be added as needed. By the time the pork is done, the cubes should be in a rich creamy sauce, with curdled milk around the edges of the pan.

Scrape all together, stir, and add 10 minutes before serving:

2 tbs. peanut butter

Stir until all the peanut butter has dissolved and the sauce is quite thick.

Serve over chunks of dry French bread, rye bread, or over rice. Accompany with a simple salad dressed with oil dressing and acidulated with lime juice or lemon juice, fresh.

X. J. Kennedy

Timeless Beef, Mushroom, Instant Coffee,
& Irish Whiskey Stew

2$1/_2$ lbs. round steak
  cut into 1-inch cubes
1 cup flour seasoned with
  dash of salt and pepper
$1/_2$ stick ($1/_8$ lb.) butter

$1/_4$ cup olive oil
3 large onions sliced thin
1 lb. whole fresh mushrooms
1 tbsp. brown sugar
1 bay leaf

3 drops Tabasco sauce
1 tbsp. Worcestershire sauce
1/4 cup Irish whiskey
1/4 cup Burgundy wine
1/2 cup instant coffee brewed strong
1 1/2 cups sour cream

Dredge beef in seasoned flour. In an iron kettle or extra-large heavy skillet or frying pan, brown the meat on all sides in the oil and melted butter. Brown the onions and mushrooms at the same time. Then throw in the remaining ingredients (holding in reserve only the sour cream) and slowly simmer for an hour and a half or more. When ready to serve, stir in sour cream and spoon it out over noodles or rice. The result is vaguely like a stroganoff, but oddly different.

Because this dish will simmer practically forever and not deteriorate, it is just the thing for anyone entertaining poets who have no idea of the time and stop for a drink along the road. The instant coffee darkens the whole brew and the Irish whiskey adds dignity. This recipe may sound like a heartless way to treat fresh mushrooms, but if you leave them whole you may be surprised how well they will stand for it.

Serves four hearty eaters.

This recipe is my variation on a friend's variation of something out of an old popular newsstand cookbook.

Carolyn Kiser

Chicken Elisofen

Make marinade:
1/3 soy sauce (preferably Tamari)
1/3 bourbon (preferably Jack Daniels)
1/3 olive oil (preferably from Lucca, Italy)

Immerse chicken parts in marinade for several hours. Then barbecue chicken on outdoor grill. (Great for the beach or the mountains!) Let the chicken *geet* good and black on the outside. And listen! It's not as expensive as it seems. In the first place, you can drink the rest of the bottle of bourbon before dinner. In the second place, the marinade can be saved and used again. ❀

Peter Klappert

Adobo (for two)

½ chicken	*2 tomatoes*
2 porkchops	*2 garlic cloves*
1 green pepper	*1 onion*
6 oz. soy sauce	*2 bay leaves*
6 oz. vinegar	*Pepper*
1 tsp. sugar	*Rice*

Mix cold the soy sauce, vinegar, bay leaves, sugar, and crushed garlic, and sprinkle with pepper. (For more salt, add soy sauce; for more sour, add more vinegar; and for more sweet, of course, add more sugar.)

In large fry pan place 1 inch of water, the chicken and the chops. Bring to a boil and add sauce. Turn down heat and cook until meat is almost cooked, then add onions, peppers, and tomatoes (in that order) so that they are still crisp when the adobo is served.

This is my "favorite" recipe for gatherings of poets (novelists, painters, even editors) and I learned it from the poet Fernando Afable. Adobo is very easy to prepare in huge quantities and relatively inexpensive (if you buy the pork in a roast and cut it up yourself). On the other hand, no one I've served it to has become famous.

Perhaps this is my second favorite recipe. I'd rather eat steamers cooked in white wine and Bermuda onion, live-broiled lobster, corn on the cob—but what honest poet can afford that?   ❋

William Kloefkorn
_____

Super Salad

Lettuce   *Artichoke hearts (in oil)*
Tomatoes   *Salt and pepper*
Garlic   *Egg*
Lemon juice

Shred the lettuce until you believe you have enough, then shred just a trifle more. You can use either romaine or solid-head lettuce; personally, I prefer to use a little of both: I like the leafiness of romaine and the solidity of the other. Quarter the tomatoes, then cut each quarter into three or four pieces. Add a clove or so of garlic, cut in very small pieces. Add a squirt of lemon juice and salt and pepper. Next, cut the artichoke hearts into pieces that are larger than a thumb-tack but smaller than a breadbox. Pour the artichoke oil all over the salad then lick off the fingers. Finally, add 1 or 2 coddled eggs (boil water, then remove water from heat; place egg in water for about 3 minutes). Toss.

This salad is marvelous. It's a variation on a recipe that my brother John copied from Vincent Price one evening several years ago while watching Price on TV. I have added a couple things to the recipe. The heart of the salad, though, is the artichoke hearts and the coddled eggs. It is a salad very easy to become addicted to, so those who take this particular salad trip should beware.   ❋

How to Make Rhubarb Wine

Go to the patch some afternoon
in early summer, fuzzy with beer
and sunlight, and pick a sack
of rhubarb (red or green will do)
and God knows watch for rattlesnakes
or better, listen: they make a sound
like an old lawnmower rolled downhill.
Wear a hat. A straw hat's best
for the heat but lets the gnats in.
Bunch up the stalks and chop the leaves off
with a buck-knife and be careful.
You need ten pounds; a grocery bag
packed full will do it. Then go home
and sit barefooted in the shade
behind the house with a can of beer.
Spread out the rhubarb in the grass
and wash it with cold water
from the garden hose, washing
your feet as well. Then take a nap.
That evening, dice the rhubarb up
and put it in a crock. Then pour
eight quarts of boiling water in,
cover it up with a checkered cloth
to keep the fruit flies out of it,
and let it stand five days or so.
Take time each day to think of it.

When the time is up, dip out the pulp
with your hands for strainers; leave the juice.
Stir in five pounds of sugar
and an envelope of Red Star yeast.
Ferment ten days, under the cloth,
sniffing of it from time to time,

then siphon it off, swallowing some,
and bottle it. Sit back and watch
the liquid clear to honey-yellow,
bottled and ready for the years,
and smile. You've done it awfully well.

Maxine Kumin

Mushroom Soup

Brown 2 cups of finely chopped mushrooms (supermarket if you must, but inky caps or chanterelles are far better) in 4 tablespoons butter. Add 1 minced onion, continue cooking. Sprinkle 3 tablespoons flour over all, stir and cook until well blended. Add 2 teaspoons chicken broth concentrate (or two of the individual packets), 1 cup yogurt, approximately 1 cup water, 1 cup milk or light cream.

Barely simmer for 30 minutes, season to taste with garlic, salt, and pepper. Leftover white wine goes well in this; substitute for the water or add to taste. I add wild sorrel leaves in season, or the hearts of young cattail stalks.

Serves 4 to 6.

This is our standard summer-fall soup. When chanterelles are plentiful, they can be buzzed in the blender first with a little wine or water; the result is a pale yellow magnificence. Wild mushrooms have far more flavor than store-bought and thus will go further, with less seasoning. 🌼

Richmond Lattimore

Gaides Pilafi
(Shrimps with Rice, Greek Style)

1¹/₂ lb. fresh shrimp   2 medium onions chopped fine
¹/₂ cup olive oil   1¹/₂ cups long grain rice

3 cups hot water	2 tbsp. parsley, chopped
1 clove garlic,	Salt and pepper
peeled and mashed	Pinch of oregano

Boil shrimp and peel them. Keep enough water to boil shrimps and rice later. Heat oil in a heavy pan, fry onion until soft. Add rice and cook 5 minutes longer. Add shrimp. Add water and seasonings. When it boils, turn heat very low, cover tightly, and cook until liquid is absorbed, 15 or 20 minutes. ✽

Laurence Lieberman

Sashimi

I've just spent a year in Japan, and while there, I positively fell in love with all the varieties of Japanese raw fish. There are two general categories of raw fish — Sashimi and Sushi. In the Sushi bars, one sits behind a long counter and points to a particular morsel of fish which is then fashioned by the master into a pattie on a ball of rice, with a dash of vinegar and mustard sauce (green wasabi) between the fish and the rice-ball. There are perhaps a dozen of different types of raw fish that can be selected for Sushi, but my favorites are awabi (abalone), tako (octopus), maguro (red tuna), and ika (squid). Sashimi is the other category of raw fish that I love.

Sashimi is sliced raw fish, served with or without a bowl of rice, with a dash of sliced radish on the side, perhaps a couple of flowers — all to be dipped in the wasabi sauce, and promptly eaten. My favorite variety of Sashimi is ajeno tataki, small silver fish — perhaps the equivalent of jack in the U.S. — sliced into fine thin strips, and covered with slices and bits of chopped chives. ✽

Thomas McAfee

Eggs McAfee

Eggs, as many as you want
Tomato, peeled and seeded, in small pieces
Mushrooms, diced
Bean sprouts (if canned, drained and washed)
Cucumber, peeled and diced
Green pepper, chopped
Onion, chopped
Sweet basil
Garlic salt
Coarse pepper
Dash of soy sauce
Dash of Tabasco
A little cream
Several drops of lemon juice

Mix all these and scramble in butter.

Claire McAllister

Baked Stuffed Sweet Oranges, Packed with Certain Tropical
Loot Such as Dates, Figs, and Coconut, Not to Mention
Chopped Cashews or Almonds, a l'Indochine

This is a classic from Saigon, overnight stop before journeying by motor car supplied by Le Bureau Central du Tourisme Indochinois, up into the amazing jungle country via Pnom Penh and Siemreap to Angkor Wat, in Cambodia; and donated by the chef of the Continental Palace Hotel as we sat in Çabaret Le Perroquet, in Saigon, studying human relationships.

For 6 oranges allow 9 pitted dates, and 8 small dried figs; also 6 marshmallows, 2 tbsp. finely chopped fresh white coconut kernel, and 2 tbsp. of finely chopped roasted cashews or unsalted almonds. Cut cap off stem end, remove pulp, and mix this last with the chopped dates, figs, and nuts. Dust well with brown sugar, after stuffing the orange shells, and bake for $^1/_2$ hour in medium oven around 350 degrees. Add 1 tsp. Cointreau to each orange, arrange on a silver platter and splash a little heated cognac over them. Serve flaming, and garnished with something appropriately tropical.

Victoria McCabe

Gruel

1 cup rice
2 cups water
Salt

Pepper
1 can chicken noodle soup

Boil the rice in salted water until it is nearly done. Add the UNDILUTED can of soup. Simmer for as long as you can stave off hunger. Season with lots of black pepper and a little salt. Eat piping hot.

Gruel is a hearty meal and is extremely cheap to make. If you can afford it, buy up a package of chicken backs to fry and eat with this gruel.

This recipe is better than it sounds.

Howard McCord

Chiricahua Scrambled Eggs

Take eight eggs, break into bowl. Add two good tablespoons of sour cream. Beat. On your chopping board, chop two spring onions up, along with three or four mushrooms (morels, if you can find some). Brown these in a skillet, maybe with some short pieces of bacon put in first, to get the grease, or just with olive oil, which I like. Open up a can of green chilis. If they're already chopped, just press in on the lid to drain them, and add; or, if they're whole, chop, after deciding whether or not you want to include the seeds, which make everything a little hotter. (If you want to get rid of the seeds, split the chili with your thumb and scoop them out. Easy to do under running water.) Now add the beaten eggs and sour cream to the skillet, and in a minute or so, put in the chilis. If you'd been wise, you would have already grated a cup of sharp cheddar cheese, and have it ready to sprinkle into the eggs. If you weren't wise, get busy. But don't overcook the eggs. Just nice and fluffy, stirred with a fork, all loose moisture gone, not hard scrambled unless you are from Ohio and don't know better. The dish should look like yellow clouds with bits of green and brown. Serves two well.

Some people have to have coffee in the morning, and if you're them, that's OK. I recommend for these eggs, however, a good champagne—Mumm's Cordon Bleu is fine; a pinot blanc, or (if you like something to charge up to the chilis, Retsina).

I won't say why these are called huevos chiricahuenses except to note the presence of a tiny town called Paradise in the Chiricahuas.

Thomas McGrath

Dog Days Soup

> $1/2$ *a cucumber per serving,*
>   *peeled, seeded, chopped*
> $1/2$ *scallion per serving,*
>   *chopped fine*

1 tablespoon green pepper
 per serving, chopped
1 teaspoon stuffed olives
 per serving, chopped
$^1/_2$ teaspoon per serving
 chopped fresh dill
$1^1/_2$ cups buttermilk per
 serving
Salt and pepper to taste
Flowers of white sorrel
 for garnish if any are handy

Put first five ingredients into the buttermilk.
Add salt and pepper.
Chill till icy. Toss on the sorrel and serve. With some good
rye bread and cheese, it's a lunch.

Nothing sacred here about quantities—more or less of anything can be used; soup can be thinned by adding more
buttermilk. Chives may be substituted for the onion, celery
for the green pepper, etc., etc.   ▓

Allen Mandelbaum

Within a Weighty Roman Poet

Agnoli with fagioli, mountainous
sweetbreads, Abruzzi kidneys, sage on slabs
of Val Vigezzo veal, Comacchio eels,
and silent nightingales from Poggibonsi;

and, in the van, the vaunt of Valtellina,
bresaola that was sliced as if by Laura,
prosciutto with Palermo's purple figs,
and culatello of Zibello, thick;

to which the Adriatic added six
crayfish, branzino broiled and oiled, with sprigs

of rosemary; and Maratea's gifts
were massive mazzancolli and thin squids;

and now his mouth would move to mozzarella,
still dripping, from the milk of Manziana's
sad buffaloes; San Gimignano sent
its tallest, transcendental tower, a tart
and pungent pecorino; apricots
were plucked in Moena; and Merano brought
blue plums, blue grapes; and Bari, bergamots;
not one need wait—he sees, he immolates;

and fountains flow with subtle Barbaresco;
and, for the fishes, brooks of cool Verdicchio;
Bassano's grappa is the last libation;
he wreathes it all with Roman eructation.

And when, beneath the moon—inedible—
above the endless altar of his table,
he has ingested all that he received
in tribute from the field and vine and sea,

will even one hendecasyllable
that he lets loose, be any more substantial?

William Matthews

Beerburgers

For 4, mix 2 pounds of ground beef with 1 tablespoon grated onion, 1 teaspoon salt, and ½ teaspoon pepper. Shape into 8 thick patties. Heat two tablespoons fat or butter in large skillet (or use two) and brown the patties on both sides.

While they're browning, mix well ½ cup catsup, ½ cup beer, 2 tablespoons each vinegar, sugar, and Worcestershire sauce, 1 teaspoon salt, dash of pepper.

When patties are brown, pour sauce over them and simmer for ten minutes.

Serve on French bread or English muffins, buttered on one side and toasted slightly. Pour remaining sauce over the burgers.

Beer or ale with these, and a green salad using lemon juice instead of vinegar in the dressing.　❋

David Meltzer

Salad Dressing

First of all it's essential to have a pint-size "Bell" mason jar. That's because the fancy "B" on the jar is the vinegar level. Pour in Japanese rice-vinegar up to the bottom edge of the "B." (You can, if you wish, mix the rice-vinegar with some wine-vinegar for a tarter flavor.) The rest of the ingredients are as follows:

> 2 *level tablespoons of*
>   *Vege-Salt (it's important*
>   *that you use this brand)*
> *$^1/_4$ to $^1/_2$ teaspoon of garlic*
>   *powder (not salt)*
> *$^1/_4$ to $^1/_2$ teaspoon of onion*
>   *powder (not salt)*
> *$^1/_2$ teaspoon of mustard*
>   *powder*
> *$^1/_4$ teaspoon of celery seed*
> *$^1/_4$ teaspoon of marjoram*
> *$^1/_4$ teaspoon of basil*
> *$^1/_2$ teaspoon (or more)*
>   *of grated Romano or*
>   *Parmesan cheese*

> *Grind in some black pepper*
> *   according to taste*
> *Sprinkle in some paprika for*
> *   color*
> *Then I add at least three*
> *   different oils:*
> *Cold-pressed Virgin Organic*
> *   Olive Oil ($^1/_6$)*
> *Cold-pressed Organic*
> *   Peanut Oil (if it's Deaf*
> *   Smith's oil, I use sparingly*
> *   as it has a deep flavor that*
> *   you might not want to have*
> *   dominating the others)*
> *Cold-pressed Organic*
> *   Corn Germ Oil ($^2/_6$)*
> *Cold-pressed Safflower Oil*
> *   ($^3/_6$)*

If you have an Osterizer you might want to put the Mason jar on it and give the dressing a blend. The idea is to be sure that all the oils reach the top of the jar before blending. The Osterizer helps to mix in the mustard powder and garlic powder. Otherwise, cap the jar and shake vigorously until everything mixes together.

For maximum flavor I suggest making the dressing in the morning and refrigerating it until dinner.

This dressing makes, keeps, and ages well.

Vassar Miller

Chili / Mac Casserole

1 cup macaroni (uncooked)
2 (16 oz.) cans chili with beans
Dill pickle slices

Cook macaroni as directed. Heat chili to boiling point. Drain cooked macaroni and combine with chili. Place in a 1½ qt. casserole. Top with pickle slices. Bake in a 375 degree oven for 20 minutes. Makes 4 servings.

I like casseroles of all kinds, especially with ground meat.

John R. Milton

From an Icelandic Friend of North Dakota

Chicken breasts	*Sour cream*
Bacon	*Mushroom soup*
Dried beef	*Salt and pepper*

Remove all bones from chicken breasts.
Twist and work the breasts, and then wrap each with a slice of bacon.
Line the bottom of a pan with dried beef.
Place the bacon-wrapped breasts on the dried beef.
Salt and pepper.
Cover the chicken thoroughly with a sauce made of sour cream and mushroom soup (half and half).

Bake at 325 degrees until tender.

When serving, garnish with pickles and olives.

Potatoes to go with the above dish:

Cut in half, lengthwise.
Bake.
Just before they are done, add either butter and salt or cheese.

Howard Moss

Meat Loaf

1 lb. chopped sirloin or round
1 medium onion chopped
1 piece of white bread,
  crumbled
1 egg
1 can of tomato sauce
  (small)

Juice of half a lemon
Pinch of thyme, marjoram,
  and rosemary
Salt and pepper
Lawry's salt or garlic powder
  (optional)

Mix all ingredients and place in a meat loaf pan. Bake at 350 degrees for forty minutes. The resulting meat loaf has a pâté-like texture and is moist.

I usually pour off most of the fat when the meat loaf is done. A pinch of sugar may be added to counteract the acidity of the lemon, depending on taste.

Howard Nemerov

Eggs Maledict

Instead of English muffins, Wonder Bread.
Instead of ham, Spam.
Instead of hollandaise, Kraft mayonnaise.
Eggs fried instead of coddled.

John G. Neihardt

Poet's Recipe for Fire-Pit Fowl Cooking

Dig a hole 3 feet in diameter and 2 feet deep. Kindle a fire in the hole and continue to add larger chunks of wood to produce a good bed of coals.

Prepare a stuffed fowl (goose, duck, or chicken). Peel a sufficient number of potatoes to be strung on a cord, as beads, to encircle the fowl. Sew the stuffed fowl and ring of potatoes in a coarse muslin sack. Wrap the bundle in a newspaper (about 1 inch thick) and secure with cord, thoroughly wrapped about it. Dunk bundle in clear water until soaked. Let drain so as not to douse fire.

Cover the coals with a blanket of long, green grass (about 2 inches thick). Place the bundle of fowl and potatoes on the grass. Cover with green grass and then heap gravel atop the grass. On top of the gravel build a fire with good wood that will burn down to coals.

Go swimming or hiking for 3 hours. Return to the fire-pit and uncover the newspaper bundle. Remove paper from bundle. Place bundle on clean area and slit open the bag, spreading the cloth around the fowl and potatoes. Dinner is now served. It will be found to be very tender.

Success of this method of cooking will depend largely on the thoroughness with which the coals have been prepared.

This is an old family recipe.

John Frederick Nims

Chicken a la Fastest Gun in the East

I like casseroles because they are easy to serve, but putting them together is something else. The most delicious casseroles—present company excluded—take as much time to assemble as a knocked-down power mower. I am therefore deeply indebted, and you will be too, to Edward W. Lowman for this recipe which I crib from his aptly named book, *The How-Not-to-Miss-the-Cocktail-Hour-Cookbook* (McKay, 1971).

2 2^1/$_2$ pound fryers, cut-up	1 cup dry vermouth
5 ounces soy sauce	1 clove garlic
^{1}/$_4$ cup sugar	1 tablespoon ground ginger

Combine all ingredients and marinate chickens in sauce overnight. When ready to cook, place chicken and half of marinade in oven-proof serving dish and bake uncovered for one hour in 325 oven. Serve with rice.

Bink Noll

Eggs Noll

Beat eight eggs together with $^1/_2$ teaspoon thyme, $^1/_2$ teaspoon marjoram, $^1/_4$ teaspoon medium grind black pepper, and palatable salting. In a large (10″ at least) frying pan sauté 2 tablespoons shallots or green onions, finely sliced, until slightly brown. Turn heat low and add egg mixture, stirring constantly until thick but not dry. Add juice of $^1/_2$ a lemon and $^1/_4$ cup chopped parsley. Still stirring, add $^1/_2$ cup dry, small curd cottage cheese. Heat through. Off flame and add $^1/_2$ cup sour cream.

Joyce Carol Oates

Easter Anise Bread

1 dozen eggs
1 tablespoon sugar for
  every egg ($^3/_4$ cup)
2 cakes yeast
$^1/_2$ cup oil
1 cup butter
1 teaspoon orange juice
1 teaspoon lemon juice
1 teaspoon anise seed
1 pinch salt
9 cups flour
Warm milk, enough to
  dissolve yeast

Beat eggs; add juices, yeast, and milk and beat slightly. Mix flour, sugar, salt, and anise. Now add to liquid mixture and mix until well blended. Let rise in bowl until nearly double in size. Punch down. Let rise again. Shape into four loaves.

Place in greased pans. Let rise and bake for 20–30 minutes at 350 degrees. ▨

Simon Ortiz

─────────────────────────────────

For All My Friends who Like It

HOW TO MAKE A GOOD CHILI STEW, THIS ONE ON JULY 16, SATURDAY, INDIAN 1971

It's better to do it outside
or at sheepcamp
or during a 2 or 3 day campout.
In this case, we'll settle
for Hesperus, Colorado,
and a Coleman stove.

1. *Ingredients*

Chili (Red, frozen, powdered, or pods. In this case, just powdered because that's all I have.) Beef (In this case beef which someone who works in a restaurant in Durango brought this morning, leftovers, trim fat off, and give some to the dog too, because he's a good guy. His name is Rex.) Beef Bouillon (5 or 6 cubes, maybe, for taste). Garlic (About 2 large cloves. Smell it to know it's good.)

Salt and Pepper (You just have to test how much.) Onion (In this case, I don't have any, but if you do have some around, include it with blessings.) Hominy (Preferably the homemade kind where, like we used to do at home, you soak them in lime water for a while until the husks wash off easy. But store-bought is okay too.)

2. *Directions*

Put chili and some water into a saucepan with beef bouillon, garlic which is diced, and salt and pepper and onion which

I don't have and won't mention anymore because I miss it and you shouldn't be anyplace without it, I don't care where.

And then put it on to barely boiling, cover, and smell it once in a while with good thoughts in your mind, and don't worry about it, except, of course, keep water in it so it doesn't burn, okay.

In the meantime, you can cut the meat (which in this case I should mention was meant for Rex the dog, but since it was leftover from just last night and it's not bad—I know cause I tasted it—that's alright but if you can afford it, cut the lean meat into less than 1-inch pieces and you don't have to measure, just cut it so it looks like cut meat).

Make sure you smell the chili in the saucepan once in a while and think of a song to go with it. That's important.

More on meat in case it's not cooked leftovers from last night. Well, you put it into a pan with tiny diced garlic with a small pat of butter and meat fat and watch it turn brown and listen to it sizzle (a delightful sound—for as long as you want just so long as it doesn't burn and set it aside and relax for a while).

Smelling and watching are important things, and you really shouldn't worry about it too much—I don't care what Julia Child says—but you should pay the most extreme attention to everything, and that means the earth, clouds, sounds, the wind; all these things go into the cooking.

And then you put everything into a pot; a cast iron one is best like the one my dad and I put a sheep's head into with rice and pieces of bread dough for dumplings and buried it in the ashes so it was cooked by the time we got home in the evening from herding sheep.

3. *Further Directions To Make Sure It's Good*

Don't forget about the chili.

Look all around you once in a while. (In this case, the La Plata Mountains in southern Colorado. It's going to rain on them and maybe here too if we're lucky.)

Don't let the Magpies get on your nerves. (Which is the case here, because Edward and Susan Magpie's kids are here by themselves. Ed and Su went someplace, maybe on vacation or to the big city—Relocation Welding School—and the kids are getting into all kinds of mischief. I throw them apples once in a while, but they're sassy and onry, chattering and swearing and laughing all the time, acting big. If you see Ed and Su, please tell them everything is okay, their kids are growing big, and you tell them to write. Maybe you'll see them around Oakland or Los Angeles. At the Indian Center.)

If there are Magpies around, make sure you invite them, saying, "I want you all to come over for dinner. We've been wondering how you've been. Your aunts and uncles and grandfather will be there." And say it with great welcoming and sincerity, and I'll betcha they'll come.

4. Waiting For It To Get Done

Oh, maybe about 2 hours for the chili to simmer and then put in the hominy and cover with water and simmercook for another 2 hours. It's also good to have a girl along, and in case she doesn't know how too good, you can teach her, slowly and surely, until she's expert. It will take more than one time, but that's okay. It's best to do anytime.

5. At Last

Well, my friends, that's all there is to it for the chili stew part, but as you well know, there is more than that too. So, good luck. And you can eat now. 🏵

Robert Peters

This is an original recipe. I dig it because of the health food ingredients.

Preheat oven to 375 degrees.

Sift into an electric mixer bowl and mix for about 2 minutes at medium speed, or mix by hand until nicely smooth:

1 cup blend of whole wheat
  and unbleached white flour
1/2 cup powdered protein
  or soy flour
3 teaspoons double-acting
  baking powder

1 teaspoon salt
1/4 cup carob powder
2 tablespoons peanut butter
2/3 cup of milk

Add and mix for 2 minutes more, scraping bowl constantly:

1 egg
1/3 cup milk
1 teaspoon vanilla

Pour the batter into greased pans and bake for about 25 minutes. Or bake in flat loaf pan for about 30 minutes.

Marge Piercy

Chuck steak or round
Mushrooms
Salt
Peppers
Grated lemon rind
(Orange rind)

Marjoram
Port (California is fine)
Cornstarch or arrowroot

Slice the fresh mushrooms lengthwise or in quarters as you like them. Sauté them quickly in 2 to 3 tablespoons of butter in a frying pan that has, available for later, a close fitting lid. Take them out and put them aside in a bowl.

Cut up your chuck steak into inch to inch and a half cubes. You want something like half a pound of meat to a person, less if you eat less or if you make the dish with lots of mushrooms.

In the same frying pan you used for the mushrooms, now sauté the pieces of chuck. You can add a little more butter.

When they are lightly browned, add the following (roughly the amount of spices for 4 servings): 1 teaspoon of salt, one eighth teaspoon of pepper, one teaspoon of grated lemon rind. Best if you use fresh zest. Just grate it right in. If you have an orange around, grate a little of that rind in also. You only use the colored part. Half a teaspoon of ground marjoram, more if you are using whole leaves or fresh. Then add $^3/_4$ of a cup of port.

Stir. Cover. Simmer an hour and fifteen minutes and then taste. Depending on how tough your meat is, you may need an hour and a half. When the meat's tender, stir your cornstarch (2 teaspoons) or arrowroot into a little more port, bring it *briefly* to a boil and when it thickens, serve it over noodles or rice.

David Ray

The Ray Steak and Kidney Pie

Chop 2 onions and brown in a heavy pan in a little vegetable oil. Cut $1^1/_2$ lbs. beef (stewing steak will do, more tender steak would be better) and 1 lb. kidneys (beef or lamb) into pieces about 1 cu. in. Coat the meat with flour and brown it in the pan with the onions.

Add salt, black pepper, 1 tablespoon (or more) soy sauce, a dash of ketchup, and a big pinch of thyme. Add about 1 cup of water and simmer until the meat is tender (add a little more water if necessary). Then pour the meat and sauce into a deep pie pan and allow it to cool until there is no steam rising.

Turn the oven to 375 degrees, and prepare the pastry as follows: in a mixing bowl put 12 oz. unbleached white flour and a dash of salt. Add 6 oz. margarine, cut it into pieces and then rub it into the flour with the fingers until there are no lumps of the margarine left. Add, a little at a time, about half a cup of cold water and mix into a stiff dough. On a floured board, roll out the dough to a little less than half an inch thick. Place the dough over the pie dish containing the meat; trim off the edges; brush with milk (to brown the pastry); and make two slits in the middle of the pastry (to allow steam to escape). Bake the pie in the oven for about 40 minutes.

NOTE: Much steak and kidney pie—and even more steak and kidney pudding—is made and eaten in England where my wife, Judy, comes from. This is her version of that traditional dish.   ❀

John Calvin Rezmerski

Mushroom Soup

Boil a gallon of water. Throw in half a dozen good sized carrots, half a dozen medium potatoes, two big onions, half a bunch of celery, a quarter head of cabbage, some parsley, salt, and pepper. Simmer all this for about two hours, then strain the vegetables out (they won't have any flavor left— feed them to your animals or throw them on your compost pile).

Keep the broth simmering while you cook 4 coarsely chopped

medium onions in a half-cup of butter until they just begin to brown. Then add a quart of sliced fresh mushrooms and cook them with the onions until they shrink. Put in about a half-cup of flour and stir it in for 3 or 4 minutes. You can add more butter if needed to keep the flour and mushroom mixture from sticking to your pan. Add this mixture to your broth, stirring it for another 3 or 4 minutes.

Add a pint of sour cream, stirring to blend. Let it simmer for a few minutes before serving. If you use whole wheat flour instead of white, use a little extra. Serve with good dark bread.

Soup is Polish soul food.

Muriel Rukeyser

Omelette Philleo

On the side of variousness in life, this is my omelette. It is made with all the combining of egg yolks and milk (or, for weight watchers, water) beaten, and egg whites and salt, beaten; the folding, slashing, and then the variation: fill with slices of cranberry sauce for a tart and various omelette. It is named for Philleo Nash, friend, former Commissioner of Indian Affairs, and Cranberry Prince.

I do not mention my pickled watermelon rind with scotch. Nor others.

Ricardo Sanchez

Chile Verde Con Carne

2 lbs. sirloin which has had all the fat, gristle, and bone removed.

2½ lbs. *hot* long green chile, if chile is not hot enough, then 4 or 5 jalapenos can also be added.

Roast the chiles in broiler part of oven so that the open flame roasts the skins; peel off skin and cut chile after it is roasted and peeled.

Meat must be rinsed a couple of times in hot running water; then it is boiled for 4 to 5 minutes; drain water and rerinse meat to degrease it, and then reboil meat in about 10 to 11 cups of water. Boil until the meat is very tender. Take meat out of boiling water and cut into chunks. Save water for Chile.

Add cut chile to water and let it simmer. Mix meat chunks with chile, add 2 to 3 cloves of garlic. Salt to taste. Chile and meat should simmer until it is barely soupy.

This traditional Chicano staple is served almost anytime; it is good with refried beans, rice, and tortillas. It is especially good with eggs (over easy) and tortillas and coffee in the morning. As with most New Mexican Chicano cuisine, flour tortillas are the thing.

Aram Saroyan

Garden Vegetable Salad (Summertime)

1½ cups bulghur
  (cracked wheat)
1½ cups boiling water
1 bunch scallions, chopped
1½ tsp. salt
¾ tsp. pepper

1½ cups chopped fresh
  parsley
½ cup chopped fresh mint
½ cup olive oil
½ cup fresh lemon juice
3–4 large tomatoes, chopped

Pour boiling water over bulghur and leave, covered, till water is absorbed (15–25 minutes).

Chop the vegetables while this is happening.
Mix bulghur and scallions together well with hands.
Stir in salt and pepper and adjust this seasoning to taste.
Add mint and parsley and mix well.
Stir in olive oil and lemon juice.
Add most of tomatoes and mix.

Surround the finished mixture with remaining chopped tomatoes, and serve with grape leaves for scooping up the mixture. This dish is good accompanied by toasted Syrian bread, black olives, and iced tea, on a hot afternoon. It is a traditional Armenian recipe, and since I am one-half Armenian, eating it for me is a kind of communion with some deep ancestral flow in my nervous system. I mean this is just delicious.

Serves about four.

Grace Schulman

Boeuf a la Bourguignonne

½ pound salt pork,	*Bay leaves*
cut into inch squares	*Thyme*
4 pounds chuck beef,	*Nutmeg*
cut into 2 inch cubes	*Parsley*
10 small white onions	*Marjoram*
Peppercorns, crushed	*Mushrooms, sliced, caps*
with mortar and pestle	*and part of stems*
Garlic, crushed, one	*Cinnamon stick (my addition)*
clove	*A good Burgundy — one bottle*
Lemon peel, grated	*Optional: cup of beef stock*

Brown salt pork in heavy pan until crisp. In the fat, sauté onions and brown beef. Transfer everything except onions into a large covered vessel (I use the Dansk model that retains the heat and flavor) and add the wine and spices. Do not remove the cover during the entire cooking time. Cover and cook for three hours. Then add mushrooms and onions and cook for another half hour.

This dish can stand while you talk with your friends. You need not worry about over-cooking. Serve with French bread, another bottle of Burgundy, wild rice, and an uncomplicated salad.

It's Sybaritic!

David R. Slavitt

Shrimp Curry (6 servings)

¹/₂ cup butter
1 medium onion, chopped
1 clove garlic, chopped
1 stalk celery, chopped
¹/₂ bay leaf
Sprig of parsley
¹/₄ teaspoon dry mustard
1 apple, peeled and diced

¹/₄ pound raw ham, chopped
2 tablespoons flour
¹/₂ teaspoon mace
1¹/₂ teaspoons curry powder
2¹/₂ cups chicken broth
3 cups peeled and veined
*   raw shrimp*

In a large saucepan, heat the butter and add the onion, garlic, celery, bay leaf, parsley, mustard, apple, and ham and cook 8 minutes, stirring occasionally. Then stir in the flour, mace, and curry powder and cook for 4 minutes longer. Add the broth and simmer, covered, for one hour. Pour the liquid off, and the solids into a blender. Blend and return to the pan, adding the originally poured off liquid. THIS IS THE BASIC CURRY SAUCE, and can be made in large quantities and frozen, to be used when needed for shrimp, chicken, lamb, or whatever.

To the sauce, add the shrimp and simmer until they turn red and are ready to eat (5 to 8 minutes, depending on size).

Serve with: hot boiled rice, pineapple chunks, mandarin orange sections, shredded coconut, peanuts, currants, mango chutney, lime chutney, Bombay Duck, papadums, crystalized ginger, and with this, India ale.

William Jay Smith

Sonja's Choucroute (*Choucroute a l'Alsacienne*)

> He abhors motorbikes and boiled cabbage;
>   Zippers he just tolerates;
> He is wholly indifferent to cribbage;
>   And cuts a poor figure on skates.
> — From "Mr. Smith"

I am thus on record in this self-portrait as heartily disliking boiled cabbage. I do; but *sauerkraut* — or *choucroute,* as the French call it — is something else. It is a great delicacy and a very ancient one. Sauerkraut in modern times has become associated with Germany, but like so many good things in this world it is supposed to have been brought back to Europe by Marco Polo. At the time of the construction of the Great Wall of China, a clever cook apparently discovered that the workmen's cabbage would keep for months when shredded and pickled in brine. If the story is true, then in the *choucroute* served *garnie* (and I wish writers of cookbooks would learn to spell it correctly — garnie not garni) with ham and sausage in Paris, where like many another American I first discovered it, the world's two great cuisines — French and Chinese — have come together. And it was, of course, in Alsace that they met. There are many complicated ways to prepare *choucroute* — by adding layers of apples and carrots, for example, but the simple, basic one I give is my favorite, that of Sonja, my Alsatian wife. Of it she says: "This is a hearty peasant dish and any sophisticated version with campagne poured over it and flambéed in front of the diner as I have seen it in certain Parisian restaurants brings nothing to the sauerkraut and is a waste of the champagne. The dish can be easily kept in the refrigerator for several days, or it can be frozen. For freezing arrange the sauerkraut in an aluminum dish topped with ham and sausages, cover and freeze. Do not freeze the potatoes; you'll have time to cook them when you heat up the sauerkraut—45 minutes if thawed beforehand, or 1 hour and a half if not." I should add perhaps that Sonja has, of course, substituted the meats most readily available here for the sausages of her native Strasbourg. The flavor of the *choucroute* seems even to improve when reheated or frozen. As my wife puts it: "The principle is *une choucroute rechauffée est toujours meilleure* (sauerkraut is always better warmed over)." The most important ingredients in this dish, my wife and I agree, are the juniper berries. They are sometimes hard to find, but get your grocer to order them. Do not attempt this recipe without them.

For 6 people:

4 pounds sauerkraut (the kind sold in bags rather than cans)
6 slices bacon
2 middle-sized onions
2 tablespoons juniper berries
1 teaspoon peppercorns
$^1/_2$ teaspoon dried thyme
3 cups very dry white wine (domestic Chablis)

2 cups beef bouillon
6 slices cooked ham (or even better, a ham butt)
6 good quality frankfurters
1 Polish sausage (about 1 pound)
6 boiled potatoes

Wash the sauerkraut carefully in a colander under cold running water. Strain. Peel and slice the onions. Line the bottom of a heavy casserole with slices of bacon. Arrange the sauerkraut in layers, alternating layers of sauerkraut with layers of sliced onions, juniper berries, and peppercorns. Pour over it 2 cups beef bouillon and 3 cups dry white wine. The liquid should be visible but should not cover the sauerkraut completely. Bring to a boil on top of the stove, then reduce heat and simmer covered for 3 to 4 hours. Check from time to time to see if there is enough liquid and if necessary add wine or bouillon. Remove from heat and allow to cool for 1 hour or more. Before serving, heat (on low heat) covered for another hour. Place the cooked ham butt or slices of cooked ham and the frankfurters on top of the sauerkraut to warm them (15 minutes).

Fry Polish sausage separately and add just before serving. Boil the peeled potatoes. On a serving dish pile the sauerkraut, arranging the ham and sausage neatly on top, surrounding the whole with the boiled potatoes. Serve with a dry white wine (Chablis or Gewurz-Traminer) or beer, adding, if you like, hot Dijon mustard.

W. D. Snodgrass

Hungarian Chocolate Palacintas Ala Snodgrass

Pancakes

For these I use a basic crepe recipe (6" crepes)
Fry the pancakes in *sweet* butter

Filling

6 oz. ground walnuts
1 teaspoon grated orange rind
3–4 tablespoons heavy cream
3–4 tablespoons Meyers
   dark rum (Grand Marnier
   or brandy)

When mixed together, the above should make a spreadable paste.

Sauce

$^1/_2$ *cup* sweet *butter*
2 *cups sugar*
1 *cup Dutch cocoa*
  (*such as Droste's*)
2 *tablespoons cornstarch*
$^1/_2$ *cup liquor* (*coordinate to*
  above choice, i.e., Meyers
  dark rum, Grand Marnier, or
  brandy)
2 *cups milk*

In a very heavy saucepan, melt the butter with the sugar and cocoa until the mixture starts to caramelize. (When caramelizing the mixture not only browns but begins to harden. The caramelized sugar will "toast" the cocoa somewhat and the butter will get a "burned butter" taste. This is what gives the sauce its characteristic flavor.)

After it starts to caramelize, immediately add the milk, stirring constantly. The hard lumps will dissolve as the liquid comes to a boil.

Dilute the cornstarch with some water (about 4 tablespoons). Pour this in a *slow* stream into the boiling syrup, stirring constantly. Remove from the fire and allow to cool to room temperature.

Dilute with the liquor you have chosen. Sauce can be refrigerated up to two weeks.

Assembling Palacintas

Place about 1 tablespoon (heaping) in the center of each crepe and fold in half, and then in half again. Place overlapped in baking dish until you use up all the filling (if you make the 6″ crepes this gives you 12 filled palacintas).

If sauce has been in refrigerator, heat until quite warm but not boiling. Pour over palacintas to thoroughly cover—in other words, let the palacintas "swim in the chocolate."

Place in a 375 degree oven for about 10–15 minutes until heated through.

Note: This is a time consuming dessert but well worth the trouble. It is extremely rich and from past experiences, I would suggest a light supper to precede it.

The result of this recipe is pretty gorgeous. It moved our good friend, Paul Theiner, the medievalist and punster, to say, "Any pal of cinta's is a pal of mine!"   ❇

Mary Ellen Solt

Viennese Almond Crescents

1 cup butter (it is very important to use butter)	*1 cup finely ground unbleached almonds (use blender or nut grinder)*
¹/₄ cup sugar	*Melted chocolate square*
2 cups flour	*1 tsp. vanilla*

Cream butter. Add sugar, flour, vanilla. Divide dough. Add melted chocolate to ¹/₂ of the dough to make it a light brown. The chocolate should not be overdone as a subtle chocolate flavor is best. Shape with fingers into crescents approximately two to three inches long and ¹/₂ inch thick. The crescents should not be too large as this is a rich delicate cookie. Bake about 35 minutes in a 300 degree oven. The cookies should not brown, but should be thoroughly baked. Cool. Roll gently in granulated sugar while cookies are still barely warm.   ❇

Helen Sorrells

Carrot Cake

2 cups sifted flour
2 cups sugar
2 cups grated raw carrots
2 cups chopped nuts
1 small can coconut
1 small can crushed
   pineapple and juice

1 teaspoon cinnamon
2 teaspoons soda
1 teaspoon salt
3 eggs
1¼ cups salad oil
1 cup white raisins

Mix well, pour in greased-floured oblong pan.

Bake at 325 degrees for 40–60 minutes.

Icing

1 cup sugar
½ teaspoon soda
½ cup buttermilk

½ cube butter
1 tablespoon white Karo syrup
1 teaspoon vanilla

Boil for 5 minutes and pour over hot cake.

NOTE: This makes a very rich cake. It can be kept very well in the refrigerator for days and days. I have served as many as 18 with it.

John Spaulding

Carrion Comfort

2 tablespoons butter
1 onion, chopped
1 pound chicken livers
2 tablespoons flour
1 cup chicken bouillon
1 teaspoon lemon juice
1 small can mushrooms

1 green pepper, chopped
1 stalk celery, chopped
⅛ teaspoon basil
⅛ teaspoon oregano
salt
pepper
parsley

90

Sauté onion in butter. Add chicken livers and cook 3 or 4 minutes. Add remaining ingredients; cook and stir 5 to 10 minutes more. Sprinkle with parsley. Serve with rice.

I serve this dish to liver-hating anemic friends of mine, one of whom left the following lines on a napkin in the bathroom before returning home:

Lines Left in the Bathroom
(after Sorescu)

The livers, pepper, onion et al.
entered my stomach
and now I am waiting
for their effect.

I feel I am turning bilious
and full of irony
(because of the liver).
That I'm filled with loneliness
and gas
(because of the pepper).

My tongue searches my mouth
for the source of the smog.
My legs search the house
for the breath freshener.

And it also seems
I am losing my hearing, and I turn
blue perhaps, perhaps sick (perhaps
because of the fly agaric).

Kathleen Spivack

Cream, Sugar, & Air

One pint heavy cream. (Make it two, if there are lots of people.)

A few tablespoons cocoa powder
Sugar to taste (if cocoa is unsweetened)
A few teaspoons powdered instant coffee (optional)

Whip the cream, fold in powdered cocoa, sugar (and powdered coffee). Put in refrigerator tray and freeze for a few hours. Makes a delicious dessert, somewhere between ice cream and mousse.

Variations: instead of cocoa or coffee, add a package of frozen or fresh strawberries (or blueberries, or canned fruit, or leftover cake crumbs). There is room for creativity here.

If the degree of inspiration is unbearable, I sometimes sprinkle a little decoration on top, before freezing.

William Stafford

Gormeh Salzee (Persian Lamb & Parsley Stew)

6 tbsp. butter
3 large bunches
  parsley, chopped
16 scallions, chopped
3 lbs. lean lamb
  cut into 1-inch cubes

Salt and pepper
Water to cover
3 lemons
5 cups canned kidney beans

1. In a heavy 4 qt. pot or Dutch oven, heat 4 tbsp. butter, add parsley and scallions, and cook slowly until parsley is dark green.

2. In a large skillet heat remaining butter, add meat and brown slowly. Season with salt and pepper.

3. Add meat to vegetable mixture, add water to cover, the juice of 2 lemons and quarters of the 3rd. Cover and simmer until meat is almost tender (approx. 1–1½ hours).

Add kidney beans, correct seasoning, and continue cooking until meat is tender.

Serve with Greek style pilaf (rice stirred into melted butter, then broiled in chicken broth with salt to taste). ✖

Ann Stanford

Chicken Tortillas

*4 whole chicken breasts
(8 pieces)
1 dozen corn tortillas,
cut in strips
1 small can Ortega
green chilies, diced*

*1 medium onion, chopped
1 lb. grated sharp cheese
1 can mushroom soup
1 can cream of chicken soup
1½ cans stock, plus
milk if necessary*

Cook chicken breasts in a covered casserole, at 325 degrees until tender. Cool, bone, break into large pieces. Reserve stock.

Brown onion gently in butter, add soups, and stock, stir until smooth. Stir in chilies.

Cover bottom of the casserole with a layer of soup. Alternate layers of chicken, tortillas, cheese, and soup. Top with cheese.

Cook covered 1 hour at 300 degrees, removing cover last few minutes for browning. Serves 8–10. Can be made ahead. Good reheated.

I like anything that has tortillas in it. This recipe I got from a friend; she got it from someone else. It is an easy casserole for dinner guests. ✖

Richard Stern

Perch a la Hyde Park

Perch	Margarine
Lemon juice	Fish Shak'N Bake
Salt	Chablis
Pepper	

Bake in 450 degree oven for 22 minutes.

Adrien Stoutenburg

Heavenly Ribs

The sherry in the following recipe is supposed to go into the ingredients, not directly into the poet. Or, if it does go directly into the poet, it is recommended that more than two tablespoons be allowed.

As for the amount of spareribs, it's hardly worthwhile to go to so much labor without using three or four pounds of these pig bones. Rule of thumb is to allow about one pound of ribs per person.

1 cup catsup	1 small clove garlic, minced
1 cup water or stock	2 tablespoons brown sugar
1/4 cup cider vinegar	2 tablespoons molasses
1 tablespoon Worcestershire	2 teaspoons dry mustard
1/3 cup soy sauce	1 teaspoon chili powder
2 tablespoons sherry	1 teaspoon ginger
1 small onion, minced	

Combine all ingredients in medium sauce pan; simmer over low heat 20 minutes. Take ribs and immerse them in the sauce, letting them marinate for an hour and a half or longer — depending on how long the poet himself or herself marinates. Remove ribs to baking dish, spoon some of the sauce over them, leaving the rest for future basting. (Above all, baste lovingly!) Oven temperature about 350 degrees to start; this can be reduced if ribs are cooking too fast. Roughly an hour and a half for thorough cooking.

Hollis Summers

Spinach Salad

$^1/_2$ lb. raw spinach washed, drained, and broken into small pieces
Combine: $^1/_4$ cup mayonnaise
 1 cup cottage cheese
 2 chopped hard cooked eggs
 4 chopped green onions
 1 oz. crumbled blue cheese
 Salt and pepper to taste

This amount serves 4 or possibly 5 people. My wife made up this salad recipe in a far ago season when we were blessed with too much spinach and too many eggs. Anything, almost anything, is willing to attach itself to the salad: the variations are determined by what we have much of. For affection's sake, however, Laura frequently abides by her original words.

May Swenson

Breakfast Bowl

1 banana (medium ripe; size, $4^1/_2$ inches long, $2^1/_2$ inches diameter)
$^1/_2$ cup Granola (various grains)
1 cup whole milk, chilled

Skin banana and slice it into plain white porcelain bowl. Add Granola, pour on milk, serve and eat with rounded (not pointed) silver spoon.

Tony Tagliabue

Risotto Alla Milanese

(My variation; I vary it a little each time.)

1 lb. of rice
A lot of good chicken broth (keep boiling)
¼ lb. or more of butter
Some red or white wine or Marsala
2 packages of saffron (Italian or Spanish)
Freshly grated Parmegiano
1 onion (chopped very fine)
Season the chicken broth with a little bit of salt and pepper

Make very good chicken broth in one big pot and keep it nearby, boiling. In another large pot, melt some butter, over medium heat, cook the small pieces of onion until they are slightly golden (*not* fried). Add the rice and saffron and a little bit of wine, stirring for about 4 minutes. Don't let the rice get brown. *Keep adding—a little at a time*—to the rice as you stir it up the boiling chicken broth—so that the rice keeps absorbing it. Stir constantly with a long wooden spoon. I keep tasting it as I make it. Cook over medium heat, uncovered; takes about 20 minutes. Don't let the rice get overcooked or too soft; and don't let the risotto finally get too dry or too soupy. A few minutes before it is ready you can add some more wine and a little grated Parmegiano and a little butter. Serve immediately with additional Parmegiano.

I like to have this plain. I like the saffron color and delicate taste; with some good wine. But you can also mix into it just before it is ready to serve some pieces of chicken and sautéed mushrooms. 🎏

James Taylor
_____

Chicken a la Taylor a la Italiano

A package of chicken breasts is easier, but if you like chicken in all its various members, you can just take the breasts from several chickens, naturally.

In any case, I use 4 to 5 chicken breasts, boned (alas, this is a chore, but a sharp, slim knife similar to a blade best for cleaning trout is an immense help).

After the meat and skin is clear of the bone, begin to simmer in a pan a mixture of butter (real), rosé wine, crushed garlic, oregano, onion salt, or diced onion.

Do not bring this to anything resembling a boiling point, rather, continue cooking over a medium flame. Turn the breasts and cover for another 5 minutes. By the time the breasts are white, very white on both sides, turn one more time shortly, then serve. The proportion for the ingredients is entirely up to the cook. Fool around with it, see what happens.

It is a very tasty and quick dinner. Goes well with cold white wine, crisp salad, and any kind of vegetable.

Garnish with good company, good conversation.

REMINDER: All food and drink is, of course, a necessary function. Yet, there is a kind of ceremony also attached. Nothing shabby or affected, but rather, grateful for the variety of tastes from an abundant selection of food, and even more from a various tradition of treatment of food. It means health, experience for the taste buds, delight in not being hungry. A good meal is a protest against poverty of all kinds and one should not feel too guilty that there are others who are cramped with the body's anger at not being fed regularly or properly. As I said in a recent poem, "Never trust a person living alone with an empty kitchen."

Randy Tomlinson

Nellie Bly's Brunswick Stew

4 pounds meat (beef, pork, chicken, game, or combination)
1 pound salt pork
3 cups diced potatoes
1 large bell pepper (chopped)
1½ cups chopped onion
1 #303 or 1 pound can tomatoes
1 #303 or 1 pound can green lima beans
1 #303 or 1 pound can corn
1 #303 or 1 pound can cut okra
1 tbsp. vinegar
1 stick butter
1 bottle catsup
¼ tsp. black pepper
¼ tsp. red pepper
Salt to taste

(Use fresh vegetables in season rather than canned)

Cook meat until done. Take out all bone, gristle, and fat. Add potatoes, bell pepper, and onion. Cook these ingredients with meat until done. Add tomatoes, lima beans, corn, okra, vinegar, butter, catsup, salt, and pepper. Continue to cook at *low* temperature until meat fibers come apart. Stir often.

Makes 5–6 quarts of stew.
Serves 16–20 people.
Freezes well—heat and serve.

Lewis Turco

Sherried Artichoke Chicken

My wife is planning my supper.
She is sharpening the serrated knife
in the crack between her incisors.

What a gross pink hummock
is her tongue testing
the edge of her kindness.

Some poor chicken
sets spreadeagled in a basket of noodles,
weeping out of its neck.

It is trying to hatch an artichoke.
But the leaves have little spears,
and they hurt.

She will feed it some sherry,
I will dine on drunken hen,
poor featherless creatures, both of us.

Peter Viereck

A Planet Omelette (for gods)

Put together infinite amounts of plutonium and uranium,
add bitters, and stir.

David Wagoner

How to Make a Highball

Select whatever brand of whiskey you prefer (or can afford).
Pour the desired amount into an appropriate glass. Add the

mixer of your choice. Shake a little. Garnish with something
pretty. Don't forget the ice.   ✺

Chad Walsh

Bread

1 cake yeast
$^1/_4$ cup lukewarm water
$^1/_4$ cup brown sugar
$1^1/_2$ teaspoons salt
2 tablespoons shortening

2 cups milk, scalded
3 cups sifted white flour
$1^1/_2$ cups rye flour
$1^1/_2$ cups whole-wheat flour

Add yeast to lukewarm water and 1 teaspoon sugar. Let
stand 5 minutes. Add salt, shortening, and remaining sugar
to milk and cool to lukewarm. Add softened yeast and the
white flour. Beat well. Add enough rye and whole-wheat
flour to make a soft dough. Knead. Let rise until double.
Punch down. Let rise a second time. Round into balls, cover,
rise 10 minutes. Shape into loaves. Rise. Bake 10 minutes at
400 degrees, then 35 to 40 minutes at 375 degrees.

I'm not much of a cook, but occasionally, when I can endure
the tasteless flaccidity of store-bought bread no more, I turn
baker. My favorite recipe is this slightly modified version of
one I secured (I think) from an ancient Metropolitan cook
book, years ago.   ✺

Eugene Warren

Bluejay Stew

This soup has the virtues of flexibility and of absorbing
oddments into new and rich combinations.

2 cups vegetables—fresh, frozen, canned or left-over (okra goes
  well with many others)
1¹/₂ cups pasta or rice
¹/₂ cup soy grits
Any meat scraps handy
5 cups liquid—meat broth, strained from vegetables or boiled
  from vegetable peelings (the last adds essential flavor and
  nutrition)

All measurements approximate.

Season appropriately for specific ingredients.

Simmer until they're cooked.

Top with garlic.

& pass the Parmesan cheese.

Robert Penn Warren
_____

Recipe

2 oz. Jack Daniels Black Label
4 oz. nonchlorinated water
2 cubes of ice
¹/₂ hour in which to meditate on the goodness of God

Marc Weber
_____

Sweet Butter-Rich, Sugar-Rich, Egg-Rich
Kolaches (Five Dozen)

2 T yeast   ¹/₂–1¹/₂ cup butter
2¹/₂ cups lukewarm water   1 T vanilla extract
4 cups sifted unbleached white   ¹/₂–1 cup brown sugar or
  flour   honey

2–8 eggs, beaten
2 cups milk, scalded and
  cooled

1 teaspoon anise extract
1 teaspoon mace
1 teaspoon nutmeg

3–6 additional cups white unbleached flour (the final amount will
vary according to how butter-, sugar-, or egg-rich you want to
make it).

Soften yeast in water. Add 4 cups unbleached white flour
and $\frac{1}{4}$ cup brown sugar. Beat well, about 100 times. Cover,
and let rise while you cream the butter with the sugar or
honey.

Stir in eggs. Fold into risen yeast sponge, along with milk,
spices, and salt. Fold in extra wheat flour as necessary to form
soft dough.

Knead five minutes. Let rise until double in volume. Punch
down, divide into individual pieces (I like them crabapple
size), shape into balls, and place on greased cookie sheet.
Flatten to $\frac{1}{2}$" height; let rise 20 minutes. Make indentation
with your thumb and place filling in it. Let rise 10 minutes.
Brush with egg or melted butter. Bake at 350 degrees for 20
minutes, or until golden brown.

If you prefer, you may roll out dough $\frac{1}{4}$" thick and cut into
squares. Place filling in center of each and twist opposite
corners together over filling.

Kolache Toppings and Fillings

Poppy Seed Topping:

2 cups ground poppy seed
1 cup brown sugar
$\frac{1}{2}$ cup honey

$1\frac{1}{2}$ cup coconut milk
  or milk
$\frac{1}{2}$ teaspoon salt

Mix well, cook slowly for 20 minutes until thick yet spreadable, cool before putting on dough.

Butter Glaze (With or Without Cinnamon):

1 cup brown sugar
¹/₂ cup unbleached white flour, sifted
¹/₃ cup butter
3 tablespoons cinnamon

Prune or Apricot Filling:

2 cups cooked, mashed, pitted prunes or apricots
¹/₂ cup honey
1 tablespoon lemon juice

Mix well until blended.
Also: cherry, apple, pineapple, peach, or berry will do for this filling.

Almond Paste:

¹/₂ lb. ground almonds
Honey to taste
2 eggs, well-beaten

Mix.

This recipe is my variation on one my mother used to make.

James L. White

In each cup put:
a dash of cinnamon,
a dash of nutmeg,

*¹/₂ teaspoon of powdered
instant coffee*

Make STRONG coffee. Instant's fine.
Heat milk.
Use equal amounts of hot milk and coffee in cups.

Have one of those wonderful little handmade cigarettes for
the nerves and sit around with friends dreaming up ways to
get a grant, quit your job, and get back to Mexico for a year.

Richard Wilbur

Herb Vinegar

Back in the middle of World War II, Sgt. Raymon S. McCray
and I found ourselves somewhere in France, provisioned
only with bread, butter, and radishes. We therefore invented
butter-and-radish sandwiches, and they were delicious.
Since then I have found that our invention, though a pure
inspiration with us, had previously occurred to others—
indeed, to entire cultures. It was the same when, some years
later, I thought of strewing curry powder on commercial
baked beans; the practice, my friends told me, was not un-
heard-of. Furthermore, although you might suppose it an
original thing to add fennel juice and foliage to a straight-up
dry Martini, I have now found that in doing so, *circa* 1952, I
simply increased the quantity of one component of dry
vermouth. Escoffier is credited with 7,000 culinary inven-
tions; I have learned to claim none.

The following is not original, then, but it's a good thing to do. In spring, make yourself a small mint-bed in a sunny place, surrounding it with half-sunken boards to prevent the mint from taking over all of nature. Divide the bed in two with another half-sunken board, and on one side, plant some spearmint dug up from a friend's garden. On the other, plant a packet of lemon balm, unless your friend can spare you some plants of that too. Lemon balm, like spearmint, is a hardy perennial, and it self-sows liberally.

While the plants are growing, save or collect a few middle-sized bottles and their tops. When the plants are big enough to be cut back, take enough to make approximately $3\frac{1}{2}$ cups of washed and scissored mint leaves, and one cup of balm leaves similarly treated. Put these into a two-quart crock, bruise them with a wooden spoon, and fill the crock with cider vinegar. Let it infuse for two or more weeks, stirring and tasting occasionally. Then pour the vinegar into bottles through a funnel containing filter paper.

You can, of course, buy your plants from any herb farm and while you are at it you can provide yourself with seeds or plants of thyme, salad burnet, tarragon, chives, basil, borage, and savory. These, singly or in various combinations, will make excellent herb vinegars when appropriately mixed with wine or cider vinegars. Many herb books offer good recipes. It is nonsense not to make one or two such vinegars each year, since it is a simple and pleasant-smelling process, and since most grocery stores offer herb vinegars in small variety and at absurd prices.

Nancy Willard

How to Stuff a Pepper

Now, said the cook, I will teach you
how to stuff a pepper with rice.

Take your pepper green, and gently,
for peppers are shy. No matter which side
you approach, it's always the backside.
Perched on green buttocks, the pepper sleeps.
In its silk tights, it dreams
of somersaults and parsley,
of the days when the sexes were one.

Slash open its sleeve
as if you were cutting a paper lantern,
and enter a moon, spilled like a melon,
a fever of pearls,
a conversation of glaciers.
It is a temple built to the worship
of morning light.

I have sat under the great globe
of seeds on the roof of that chamber,
too dazzled to gather the taste I came for.
I have taken the pepper in hand,
smooth and blind, a runt in the rich
evolution of roses and ferns.

You say I have not yet taught you

to stuff a pepper?
Cooking takes time.

Next time we'll consider the rice.

Miller Williams

Sweet Corn Bread

1 cup fine-ground   1 egg
   yellow corn meal   1 cup milk

1 cup all-purpose flour
$^1/_4$ cup sugar
4 teaspoons baking powder
$^1/_2$ teaspoon salt
3 or 4 tablespoons bacon drippings or liquid vegetable oil

Preheat oven to 425 degrees.

Mix with spoon the cornmeal, flour, sugar, baking powder, and salt. In another small bowl, beat together the egg and milk and then add drippings or oil to egg and milk.

Pour liquid ingredients, while stirring, into flour mixture. Beat with spoon until mixture is thoroughly blended.

Put about 1 tablespoon shortening in an $8^1/_2$″–9″ heavy black iron skillet and heat in oven. Get the skillet good and hot. Pour off excess oil.

Pour corn bread mixture into hot skillet and bake for 20–25 minutes.

This recipe has been in my family for years. Don't leave off the preheating of the skillet!

Harold Witt

Esther Hewitt's German Potato Salad

8–10 medium size, new red potatoes
4 onions
$^1/_4$ cup ($^1/_2$ cube) oleo or butter
$^1/_3$ lb. sliced bacon
$^1/_2$ cup cider vinegar
$^1/_2$ cup water
1 tablespoon sugar
2 tablespoons cornstarch
Salt and pepper

Boil potatoes until just tender (do not overcook). Drain, cool, peel, and slice into a large bowl. Lightly salt and pepper.

Chop onions and fry slowly in oleo or butter until tender (not brown). Put fried onions over sliced potatoes and gently mix.

Cut bacon in one inch pieces and fry. Add the vinegar, water, and sugar to cooked bacon and bacon fat.

When mixture begins to boil, add the cornstarch mixed in a little water. Stir until thickened. Pour sauce over potatoes, and onions, and gently mix. Add seasoning to taste.

The salad tastes better served warm. Delicious with ham.

This is an old German recipe handed down from my Milwaukee mother-in-law, Esther Hewitt, to my wife, and, maybe, to my daughters, if they aren't liberated from the delights of the kitchen.

Charles Wright

An Old-Fashioned Favorite Dessert Recipe

³/₄ cup butter
1 cup sugar
3 eggs
1¹/₂ teaspoons soda
1 cup buttermilk
2 cups flour

1 teaspoon baking powder
1 teaspoon cinnamon
¹/₂ teaspoon nutmeg
1¹/₂ teaspoons vanilla
³/₄ cup wild blackberry
preserves

Cream butter and sugar till very light. Beat in eggs 1 at a time. Add soda to buttermilk. Add sifted dry ingredients alternately with buttermilk to sugar and butter mixture. Add vanilla and blackberry preserves. Bake in 2 greased layer pans at 350 degrees until center springs back when touched. When cool, turn out and frost.

This dessert recipe is not exactly my favorite, but my favorites are something I usually do not eat at home, so I send the dessert recipe. ❀

Paul Zimmer

Zimmer's Old-Fashioned Summer Day Mud Cakes

I haven't cooked anything since I whipped up a mud pie when I was eight years old. The recipe was: mix well some good backyard dirt with a half cup of water from the garden hose and a good hawking of spittle. Shape into a patty and sprinkle well with sand from an anthill, dotting with a dead cricket. Put out in the sun for half the day and then feed it to your father when he comes home tired from work. If he won't eat it, look disappointed, as if you plan to rob banks when you grow up because of his neglect. ❀

INDEX

113

115